BRITISH RAJ TO AMRIT KAAL

EIGHT PIVOTAL INITIATIVES THAT TRANSFORMED INDIA

GAZ BISHT

Vitasta

Published by
Renu Kaul Verma
Vitasta Publishing Pvt Ltd
4348/4C, Ansari Road, Daryaganj
New Delhi - 110 002
info@vitastapublishing.com

ISBN: 978-81-19670-36-9
© Gaz Bisht
First Edition 2025
MRP ₹450

Edited by Abhijit Baroi
Layout & Cover Design by Rohit Gautam
Printed by Chaman Enterprises, New Delhi

Contents

To the unsung heroes
—the 'Sherpas'—
who relentlessly pursued several pivotal initiatives
that weaved the tapestry of the nation's progress

◆ ◆ ◆ ◆ ◆ ◆

FOREWORD

'Amrit Kaal' (the 'Nectar Era') is the current Indian Prime Minister Narendra Modi's ambition for the first centenary of his country after Independence. Introduced in 2021 as a catchphrase of the Modi government, Amrit Kaal has caught the imagination of New India, encapsulating the country's pent-up demand for prosperity, development and the good life—in a word, normalcy. Amrit Kaal is as much an expression of national pride as of national aspiration. It represents the desire of all Indians to play a role in the world commensurate with their talents, their contributions and (it must be admitted) their numbers. It means an India that Indians want to live in, not an India that Indians have to live in because they are unable to obtain a visa to live somewhere else.

The New India of confident technologists, diplomats and gurus of all stripes striding the world stage is, ironically, a return to a very old India. In the millennia before the Turkic and British conquests of the country, 'India' was a byword for wealth and wisdom, both in the Western and in the Eastern imagination. It was the exotic land that even Alexander the Great could not conquer; the home country of the holy Garuda bird of southeast Asia; and the source of enlightenment in the Chinese classic novel

Journey to the West. There are no meaningful economic statistics for the pre-modern era, but it is worth considering that Indian trade was the foundation of the affluence of ancient Alexandria. Why Alexandria? Because from the time of Darius the Great until the Muslim conquest of Egypt, there was a canal linking the Red Sea to the Nile, meaning that goods from India could be transported by ship directly from the Malabar Coast to the Mediterranean basin.

But that old India has almost vanished from our collective historical memory. Through 750 years of first Turkic and then British plunder, India went from being famous as a source of wealth to being notorious for famine and poverty. Much is made of the fact that the Turkic colonisers of north India were Muslim and it is sometimes emphasised that the later British colonisers were Christian, but it is probably more important that both were foreign. Neither cared much for the welfare of the people they ruled.

Independence and democracy brought India its first opportunity for self-determination in centuries, but the country was starting from near-zero. Even the famous Indian Railways inherited by the new country had a track-mileage only twice that of tiny England and Wales—and of much lower quality.

In such constrained circumstances, day-to-day government is itself a challenge, without the additional burden of planning for a better future. But better futures don't make themselves and visionary leaders have repeatedly gone far beyond the status quo to implement radical improvements. In *British Raj to Amrit Kaal*, Gaz Bisht describes eight such pivotal initiatives that made modern India. These were the incorporation of the former princely states, the establishment of the Indian Institutes of Technology, the generation of a 'green revolution,' the development of nuclear weapons, the creation of a framework for public-private infrastructure partnerships, the implementation of the Aadhaar system of national identification numbers, the spread of financial inclusion and the ending of open defecation.

In each of these eight cases, political leaders turned to expert sherpas to reach goals that the government bureaucracy either could not or would not accomplish on their own. Although it is not his first case study, Bisht's paradigmatic case is probably the collaboration between Chidambaram Subramaniam, the erstwhile Union Minister for Food and Agriculture and the agronomist M S Swaminathan that led to the green revolution. The keys to their success were commitments to working "on all aspects of the crises simultaneously rather than sequentially," to meeting in person with those affected by their policies "rather than relying on bureaucrats and their reports," and to demonstrating with full-scale working models that their policies would work in practice and not just in theory. Early wins generated envy among those who had not yet had the opportunity to participate, driving demand for inclusion that rapidly overcame resistance to change.

With the possible exception of Bisht's first case study (the accession of the princely states to Independent India), all of the other cases closely follow the Subramaniam-Swaminathan template. Pie-in-the-sky ideas became nationwide practical realities because once one constituency had a taste of a better way of doing things, other constituencies demanded to be let in on the benefits. For this politics of envy to work, a reform has to first be fully up and running for someone, not stuck in a stage of partial completion for everyone. Bisht focuses on the politician-sherpa relationship as crucial, but it may be that this sequencing is the more important part of the formula. Either way, the eight pivotal initiatives featured by Bisht certainly make for valuable case studies with the potential to inspire future reformers. They should be studied and emulated, not only in India, but in all resource-constrained countries.

Bisht is convincing in drawing conclusions from his case studies, but he is perhaps wrong to see in his results a template for Amrit Kaal. As India grows in capacity (and in confidence), the need for these kinds of pivotal policy initiatives will eventually pass. India will soon have the world's third largest economy and serious structural poverty in India will likely be eliminated by the end of the decade.[1] India has a surfeit of technological talent and is able to raise funds for infrastructure investment on global markets at commercial rates. The bureaucratic efficiency of Indian civil administration is still low, but by all accounts, it is rapidly increasing.[2] Bisht argues that to achieve Amrit Kaal, India "must adopt a deliberate policy to drive AI innovation and adaptation',' but it is not at all clear that a government initiative in this area will promote, rather than retard, the progress of private industry.

Bisht concludes *British Raj to Amrit Kaal* with a series of proposals for five new pivotal policy initiatives covering AI-powered classrooms, childhood stunting, green cities, health care equity and environmental recovery. No doubt all of these would be good things to accomplish. But pivotal initiatives of the kinds featured by Bisht work best in environments where it is necessary to leapfrog existing practices to establish entirely new operating norms. In each of these five areas, it may be that the continuous improvement that accompanies economic growth will better serve India than any strategic intervention by government ministers and their hand-picked sherpas. It may be, perhaps, that the real meaning of Amrit Kaal is that India can now meet its governance challenges through the ordinary, rather than extraordinary, tools of government.

Whether Bisht is right or wrong about the continuing need

for pivotal initiatives, there is no doubt that the eight policy successes featured in *British Raj to Amrit Kaal* should serve as models for other developing countries to follow on their own paths to Nectar Eras. Though his book naturally focuses on India, Bisht's analyses might most profitably be read in places such as sub-Saharan Africa, central Asia and the Pacific islands. They show how a looted and conflict-torn country can pick itself up by the bootstraps and, with little or no international assistance, transform important aspects of national life for the better. Thus, in addition to tracing the titular path from 'British Raj to Amrit Kaal,' Bisht's book also serves as a guide for India to progress from Amrit Kaal to *Vishwaguru*—from fostering one's own Nectar Era to becoming a World Teacher.

Gaz Bisht's *British Raj to Amrit Kaal* is an important book and is in fact by far the best of the new crop of books to address Narendra Modi's 'Amrit Kaal' commitment. Where other books serve up Modi hagiographies or unremitting Indian hypernationalism, Bisht offers serious historical analyses leading to practical policy recommendations. He uses a business viewpoint to identify the determinants of policy successes, looking beyond the specifics of individual cases to isolate the factors that really mattered in the past and can be replicated in the future. For these insights, Bisht's *British Raj to Amrit Kaal* should be widely read not only within India, but perhaps more importantly, throughout the developing world.

India has not yet reached the centrality in the global economy that it enjoyed before the coming of colonialism, but it has come a long way from the depths of domination it endured for 750 years under foreign rule. Indians are now on the threshold of enjoying life in a 'normal' country, not one torn by conflict or oppressed by poverty, but one in which everyone has an equal opportunity to live and flourish. If Amrit Kaal means anything, it should mean that the son of a railway station tea seller can grow up to be prime minister and the daughter of a tribal farmer can grow up to be president. By those tests, India has already entered its Nectar Era. The eight pivotal initiatives described in *British Raj to Amrit Kaal* will continue to play an outsized role in turning this historical ambition into reality by 2047.

Salvatore Babones

American sociologist and associate professor at the University of Sydney

***

INTRODUCTION

Starting from here, the journey of the next twenty-five years is the 'Amrit Kaal' of a new India. The fulfilment of our resolutions in this Amrit Kaal will take us till 100 years of Independence.

— Prime Minister Narendra Modi
15 August 2021, Independence Day Speech

'Today I have come to tell you, the whole country, that we have decided to withdraw all three agricultural laws,' Narendra Modi, Prime Minister of India, stated in an address to the nation on 19 November 2021.[1]

Long-time watchers of Indian affairs, including myself, immediately felt a sense of déjà vu. Backtracking and watering down of policies have indeed been common occurrences in politics and policymaking in India since Independence. They have led to confusion and uncertainty and made it difficult to achieve long-term policy goals.

However, the withdrawal of much-needed farm laws was even more alarming and raises the central question as to how the government would be able to implement the tough policy decisions necessary during the Amrit Kaal period to lay the groundwork towards making India a developed nation.

All agricultural economists worth their salt had presented a solid case for these new farm laws. Gita Gopinath, the Chief Economist of the International Monetary Fund, said the 'farm bills and labour bills are very important steps in the right direction.'[2]

Salvatore Babones, sociologist and professor at the University of Sydney, Australia, supported the farm laws and said that the reforms would transform Indian agriculture from a 'locally managed rural economy into a modern national industry.'[3]

Indian agricultural experts such as Ashok Gulati[4] wrote several articles in reputed newspapers in support of the laws.

Most TV debates demonstrated general support for the laws in the months leading up to the decision.

The new laws were designed to improve the efficiency of the agricultural sector and boost food production. The government had presented these laws as reforms akin to the 1991 opening of the Indian economy to global markets.

The withdrawal of the laws, when seen in light of the several promises that the current government made to the farmers during the election campaign, is perplexing at best. They had promised to double farmers' income and to provide them with a better deal.

The laws that were withdrawn were seen as a major step towards fulfilling these promises.

THE WITHDRAWAL of farm laws was a watershed moment in the second term of the Modi government who had returned with an increased majority in the Parliament. It raised an important question—is democracy (and the process of forming new laws and Acts through the Parliament) alone sufficient to deliver on the real intent of progress in the largest democracy?

The situation seems to be grimmer in the 'oldest democracy.'

Barack Obama won the presidency of the United States on a similar theme to Modi—optimism and sincere promises. Like Modi, Obama presented himself as the candidate of change, pledging to fundamentally transform domestic policy in many areas of life—health care, environmental regulation, immigration law, labour policy and the financing of higher education.

The majority of Americans said, 'Well, maybe we can.'

But a sense of despair set in less than halfway into his first term, with many now seem to be concluding years later, 'Well, maybe not ....'[5]

The election of Trump in 2016 as well as the unprecedented mob attack on the United States Capitol in January 2021[6] compelled many to ask whether democracy indeed delivers when contrasted with the staggering growth of China, particularly since 2000.[7] Furthermore, it seems that Indian democratic dysfunction compares unfavourably to China's seemingly purposeful and effective authoritarian government.[8]

With this backdrop, it becomes a central question whether India and its decision-makers will be able to achieve substantially different results during the Amrit Kaal period, or whether the next twenty-five years will be a damp squib.

SINCE BECOMING a nation-state seventy-five years ago, India has been unique among major democracies in some striking ways. She has been and still is the world's largest democracy, and at the same time, has struggled to achieve substantial economic progress. Due to several factors, including a protectionist economic policy, lack of investment and widespread corruption, India's economy grew at a slow pace, derisively known as the 'Hindu rate of growth,' during the first forty years after its Independence.[9]

In 1991, India began to implement economic reforms, which led to a period of rapid economic growth. However, despite this progress, India still faces significant challenges, including poverty, inequality and unemployment.

Most well-meaning Western heads of state and business leaders sincerely want India to succeed because it is a vibrant democracy with enormous potential. However, India has seemed to be unable to get its act together ever since becoming a free nation.

Since Independence, India has had twenty-two governments headed by fifteen Prime Ministers (PMs). Each PM and their government served in completely different time periods and each of them faced unique challenges and problems. While India's PMs have come from diverse backgrounds, each in his or her position as 'first among equals' has sought to guide the country along what they believed to be the correct path of nationhood.

In the past seventy-five years, numerous policies were formulated and implemented for uplifting the lives of its citizens.

However, a comparison with its giant neighbour indicates that the policies of the past seventy-five years, drafted and implemented by the various governments, haven't worked. While the Chinese and Indian economies were almost equal as recently as 1990, China's nominal gross domestic product (GDP) reached $17.7 trillion in 2021, which is about 5.7 times that of India's $3.1 trillion.[10]

One of the potential reasons that has been repeatedly sighted by several experts is that India is so massive and so hugely diverse. In addition, with several states as large as the size of Mexico with huge populations that are bolted together in the 'quasi-federal' setup, governance is a unique challenge.[11]

FORTUNATELY, THINGS are looking up for India—again! As recently as May 2022, *The Economist* ran a cover story about India, asking whether this was the country's moment—and concluded that yes, it probably is.[12]

In the same year, Stanford economist and Nobel Prize laureate Michael Spence declared that 'India is the outstanding performer now,' noting that the country 'remains the most preferred investment destination.' Spence expressed confidence in India's economic trajectory over the next decade.[13]

India Today, the leading magazine and news house in India, organised a two-day conference in March 2023 with the central theme being 'The India Moment.'[14]

Every expert who participated in the conference had a similar view: from the economy to geopolitics to entertainment to sports, the country is making its presence felt in every field.

Whilst these reports and opinions might cast a warm glow on Indian politicians and policymakers, will India be able to sustain it for the next twenty-five years? Or falter as she has done so many times? How should India go about the next twenty-five years to achieve the objectives of Amrit Kaal? A comparison with developed countries shows that the government has a long road ahead if it wants to turn India into a developed economy within the next twenty-five years.[15]

Most opinion makers as well as economists have been recommending to follow the 'China model' and/or the Four Asian Tigers' approach with significant growth in manufacturing, in particular focusing on the exporting of manufactured goods.[16]

However, the current times are quite different to the period when these countries started their journey of economic prosperity.

More recently, a new well-meaning recommendation includes focus on highly-skilled services and manufacturing centred on innovative new products and to make India a ferment of ideas and creativity (Rajen & Lamba, 2023).

Others such as S N Subrahmanyan, who runs Larsen & Toubro, argues for redefining the traditional contours of development with a focus on sustainable infrastructure and broad-based skill development.[17]

However, these are merely broad-brush strokes and provide 'motherhood and apple pie' guidance.

ONE OF the basic premises of this book is that, contrary to the popular pessimism surrounding India's ability to deliver, India has done remarkably well in the past seventy-five years, particularly in response to the several crises that she has faced. The key to this success has come from defining and executing what is referred to throughout this book as 'pivotal initiatives.'

A pivotal initiative differs from government policy in several ways. A government policy is typically aimed at a specific issue and goes through as a typical bill (or a proposed law) that passes through several stages in both of the Houses of Parliament. Once passed, the responsibility of effective implementation of the policy lies with bureaucrats and government officials; often, at this stage, it either fails in meeting the objectives or gets watered down (or even reversed) by subsequent governments.

In contrast, a pivotal initiative is a more holistic solution in many ways. It often comes about out of necessity as a response to various interrelated crises. The formulation and implementation of the initiative doesn't follow a fixed structure (like in government), but rather tends to be shepherded through by a tireless 'sherpa'—who possesses a deep understanding of the crises and also displays doggedness to overcome the inevitable obstacles that arise in trying to push the initiative through. Finally, once implemented, the initiative is so transformative that it creates a step change in the progress of the nation, and often other beneficial policies are enacted around or on top of it.

Take, for example, Aadhaar.

India implemented a pivotal initiative of building the world's largest biometrically secured national identification system, which is discussed later in this book. Nandan Nilekani, often known as the man who gave India 'Aadhaar' was, in fact, the 'sherpa' who had a deep understanding of the crisis and a vision for a solution. More importantly, he displayed doggedness to overcome several obstacles that arose during the long process of nearly six years.

Once completely rolled out, Aadhaar was linked to bank accounts that facilitated Direct Benefit Transfers (DBTs) of welfare subsidies directly into accounts of the poor. It has been successful in controlling the leakage of government subsidies and created the world's largest and most effective financial inclusion by bringing banking to the bottom of the pyramid. The Aadhaar initiative has been instrumental in designing and instigating another pivotal initiative—the Pradhan Mantri Jan Dhan Yojana (PMJDY)—that is also covered in detail later in this book.

Pivotal initiatives have worked in the 'oldest democracy'—the United States of America.

In the early 1960s, when John F Kennedy was the president of the USA, the Soviet Union had taken a significant lead over the USA in its space programme. Kennedy did not draft a new law as a response to speed up the country's efforts in space technology, but challenged the nation in his address at Rice University on 12 September 1962 to claim a leadership role in space. The USA subsequently landed two men on the Moon before the end of the decade due to the focused efforts of NASA.[18] Furthermore, this success subsequently gave rise to several new industries related to space technology.

The same conclusion can be drawn from the 'New Deal' initiative of President Franklin D Roosevelt in the 1930s in response to the Great Depression. During the crisis, the United States experienced an economic collapse. This gave rise to deep unemployment and widespread social unrest. President Roosevelt implemented a series of initiatives, rather than making new laws to tackle the crisis, widely known as the 'New Deal.' It was centred around infrastructure projects, public works initiatives and social welfare programmes. These initiatives helped to lift the country out of the depression and laid the foundation for a massive post-war economic prosperity that continued for decades.

In the seventy-five years since independence, India has implemented eight pivotal initiatives in response to crises of monumental proportion. Lessons from these initiatives could provide a roadmap and a vital link for new pivotal initiatives during Amrit Kaal. This book discusses these eight pivotal initiatives comprehensively and highlights shining examples of excellent delivery.

The success of Amrit Kaal, to a large degree, will depend on the ability of politicians and policymakers to 'remember the past to see the future.'

This book shows that India's success stories extend across various political regimes, economic landscapes, and social contexts during the past seventy-five years, and demonstrates India's resilience and ability to deliver positive outcomes through its inherent adaptability and willingness to embrace change.

This book examines pivotal initiatives that have transcended these boundaries and underscore the importance of focusing on areas that address fundamental challenges and seek long-term benefits rather than short-term gains. These initiatives, by their very nature, require a broad vision and a willingness to engage in long-term delivery.

In a way, the success of these initiatives gives the golden glow for the Amrit Kaal.

In the eight chapters ahead, I will introduce you to these pivotal initiatives, and attempt to weave together key lessons and a broad framework that not only made them effective in solving the crises that these initiatives were designed to solve, but also laid a foundation for several new opportunities beyond the initial crises. I aim to show how committed, selfless individuals who were the 'sherpas' of these initiatives overcame the most intimidating obstacles.

While the initiatives in this book are diverse and span across various time periods over India's seventy-five years of Independence, they all share one thing in common: they were all driven by a deep passion to make a difference. The stories in this book are inspiring and thought-provoking. They show us what is possible when people are driven by a passion for change. Whether it was uniting more than 565 princely states into a country in record time, or making India open defecation-free in five years, the 'sherpas' who led the charge were all motivated by a desire to make their country a better place.

In addition to passion, these individuals also had a strong sense of resilience. They were not deterred by the challenges they faced, but instead used them as an opportunity to learn and grow. The resilience of Nandan Nilekani who was the 'sherpa' of the Aadhaar initiative, is a case in point. He smartly worked around the then-powerful Home Minister, P Chidambaram, who was not supporting Aadhaar. Nandan was also willing to take risks and experiment, which is often necessary for success, when he targeted to provide an Aadhaar card to over 200 million Indians in the first six months, rather than unproductively arguing with Mr Chidambaram.

The book emphasises the need for collaboration and collective action, bringing together politicians, policymakers, community leaders, journalists and engaged citizens to drive meaningful discussions and transformative action, like in the case of the Swachh Bharat Abhiyan initiative.

This book's target audience aligns with this collaborative approach, encompassing a diverse group of individuals who play crucial roles in shaping India's future. Politicians and policymakers can utilise the insights gained from understanding the context of various initiatives to craft effective policies that foster development. Community leaders can mobilise and empower their communities to actively participate in the development journey. Journalists can inform and engage the public, fostering awareness and promoting responsible citizenship. Engaged citizens can actively contribute to the development process by voicing their concerns, participating in civic initiatives and holding their leaders accountable.

By bringing together these diverse perspectives and expertise, this book can serve as a catalyst for meaningful discussion and transformative action. It can spark dialogue, generate new ideas and encourage collaboration among stakeholders—ultimately contributing to India's progress towards becoming a developed nation.

But before we get to them, let's try and unpack these initiatives to find the common threads that shine brightest—with the aim of generating a broad template for policymaking and implementation during Amrit Kaal—so that India indeed does become a developed nation when it celebrates its 100 years of Independence!

A Framework for Amrit Kaal Wei Ji: A word for both crisis and opportunity.

In a speech in 1959, John F Kennedy pointed out that 'when written in Chinese, the word 'crisis' is composed of two characters—one represents danger and one represents opportunity.'[19] This characterisation of the word 'crisis' has a lot of parallels to India's experience as a nation over the past seventy-five years. The eight pivotal initiatives that are explored in this book demonstrate how India has turned crisis into opportunity.

Crises are a rather common occurrence in the journey of every country. Furthermore, an inevitable byproduct of a globalised world is that they get more attention than ever, given the 24/7 news cycle that exists today.

India has had her own share of crises since becoming a nation-state in 1947.

The eight chapters in this book show, without any shadow of a doubt, that India has risen to overcome every crisis, time and again.

In fact, India's birth as a country was out of a crisis of many dimensions—political, economic and humanitarian.

Whether it was convincing more than 565 princely states to unify as a nation, or showing deep resolve to implement a green revolution through modern farming practices and high yield seeds—India demonstrated what it takes to convert a peril into an opportunity. Today, India is a united and prospering country with surplus grain being exported. No Act or law passed by Parliament would have produced similar wide-ranging opportunities than what was accomplished by a pivotal initiative.

More recently, the crisis of open defecation had become an issue of national shame as well as a serious safety concern, particularly for women. Several policies and laws were framed to tackle the issue since the middle of the 1980s, but it took the

Swachh Bharat Abhiyan—a pivotal initiative—to solve it once and for all. This initiative has improved solid waste management and has also created an industry around it.

The bottom line is there are known crises as we head into Amrit Kaal, and there will be several unknown crises in the coming twenty-five years. India must try and meet them uncompromisingly by launching new pivotal initiatives that will not only resolve the crisis, but also create new opportunities that will propel India towards Viksit Bharat.

A selfless, dedicated 'sherpa' takes every initiative to the finish line.

The sherpas—the unsung heroes of the Himalayas—are known for making others achieve their dreams by supporting them with their enormous experience, patience and humility. Each of the eight pivotal initiatives had one thing in common—a sherpa who was selfless, dedicated and demonstrated doggedness to complete the initiative against all odds.

These eight examples serve as a testament to the sherpas, their unwavering spirit and selfless dedication to others and their unwavering commitment to overcoming challenges. Their stories will be sure to inspire Indian policymakers as well as politicians to embrace challenges with determination.

As the first pivotal initiative shows, V P Menon, who was a 'sherpa' working alongside Sardar Patel, achieved a near-impossible target of merging more than 565 princely states into a nation-state in record time. He crisscrossed the country to convince the princes of these states, despite poor health, and was doggedly committed to finding a solution when challenges arose along the way.

Similar selfless dedication could be seen in Parameswaran Iyer, who left his high-profile job with the World Bank in Vietnam and led the Swachh Bharat Abhiyan to its ultimate success. He was instrumental in changing the working culture of his own Ministry of Drinking Water and Sanitation.

All the sherpas had the unwavering trust of the political leaders during the implementation phase of these initiatives, whether it was Menon with Sardar Patel, Nandan with Manmohan Singh or Iyer with Narendra Modi.

A pivotal initiative overrides political compulsion and provides continuation in governance regardless of which party gets elected.

One of the key features of democracies is the inevitable impact on policies due to leadership change on account of an election outcome, especially in terms of budgetary allocations.[20]

The descent of US politics and governance into pervasive paralysis, conflict and sheer mediocrity are seemingly intrinsic shortcomings of democracy.[21]

In India's seventy-five-year history, there have been twenty-two different central governments and budgetary allocation changes to previous government policies has been a central theme. For example, the current government has reduced funding for the Mahatma Gandhi National Rural Employment Guarantee Act (MGNREGA), often referred to as a 'scheme.'[22,23]

In India, petty powerbrokers within ruling parties and small-minded coalition partners have chopped and changed most of the policies of the previous government after every election. Every five years, there have been new policies, or old policies have been rehashed by incoming governments, repackaged towards their support base. This has led to a lack of continuity and coherence in policymaking, which has in turn hampered the delivery of government programmes and policies.

Compromised policymaking and implementing always falls short, whether in India or in the US. Ten years after the Affordable Care Act (ACA) was signed into law in the US, it has failed to live up to its promises to reduce health care costs, increase access, and improve health care quality. With its dramatic premium increases, decreased access, and reduced choice in insurer markets, the ACA has, in fact, done the exact opposite.

In the US, Trump's election proved to be a death knell to the ACA. The Trump administration's efforts to sabotage the ACA and their consequences received detailed attention in a recently released Brookings book.[24]

The successful implementation of the pivotal initiative of the Green Revolution not only turned India into a self-sufficient food producer but ultimately made India a grain-exporting country. Contrast the withdrawal of the three well-meaning farm laws (a government decision) in 2021 with the Green Revolution success (a pivotal initiative) of the mid-1960s and I rest my case!

Infrastructure building in India did not take off until the initiative of attracting funds under the public-private partnership (PPP) model was worked up by Gajendra Haldea, who worked as an adviser to the Deputy Chairman, Planning Commission India. He was the true 'sherpa" who initially learnt the financial and legal obligation himself before guiding the ministries on the intricacies of the model contract law.[25]

The PPP initiative has continued across four governments.

The Aadhaar pivotal initiative not only survived three governmental changes, but was actually pushed forward with greater urgency by successive governments. It was conceived by Atal Bihari Vajpayee (PM in 2000)[26], developed by the Manmohan Singh government and adopted wholeheartedly by the Modi government.

The Modi government has given Aadhaar a life of its own

by linking various other governmental schemes to it such as bank accounts.

Pivotal initiatives lead to good governance and new opportunities.

Democratic governance lays emphasis on responsive, effective processes that deliver to the public without any opportunity for corruption and malpractice.

India's experience shows successful execution of a pivotal initiative that has paved the way for building effective public processes and has helped reduce corruption and improve public service delivery to her citizens. India has completed two crucial pivotal initiatives in the past nine years—a national identity card, Aadhaar, and financial inclusion for every citizen in the form of the PMJDY. These initiatives have led to effective delivery of government services and payments and have reduced corruption and leakage to a large extent.[27]

The bedding down of these two crucial initiatives has helped establish another pivotal initiative that is likely to change the face of digital commerce. The Open Network for Digital Commerce (ONDC) initiative, currently being worked on, aims to create new opportunities, curb digital monopolies and support micro, small and medium enterprises by helping them join online platforms.[28]

What is encouraging is that ONDC has a 'sherpa' in Nandan Nilekani—who led the Aadhaar initiative. This is an important step in giving the initiative the best chance possible to become the first pivotal initiative completed during the Amrit Kaal period.

GIVEN THE current global situation, coupled with a hostile northern neighbour, abandoning hope for a positive outcome during Armit Kaal certainly is tempting.

However, despair is unproductive and unnecessary.

As the following chapters will show, none of the current or future challenges are actually insurmountable. The solution is already out there. India just has to know where to look for inspiration and find an effective template.

***

Union of Princely States with India

Birth of a Nation

Long years ago, we made a tryst with destiny, and now the time comes when we shall redeem our pledge, not wholly or in full measure, but very substantially. At the stroke of the midnight hour, when the world sleeps, India will awake to life and freedom. A moment comes, which comes but rarely in history, when we step out from the old to new, when an age ends, and when the soul of a nation, long suppressed, finds utterance...

...The ambition of the greatest man of our generation has been to wipe every tear from every eye. That may be beyond us, but so long as there are tears and suffering, so long our work will not be over. And so we have to labour and to work, and work hard, to give reality to our dreams. Those dreams are for India, but they are also for the world.

—Jawaharlal Nehru
Indian Prime Minister, August 15, 1947

A NEW NATION, whose potentialities can only be guessed at, is rising in Asia—in a plastic Asia that may yet, in sure hands, be shaped into a mould for the future of the world.[1]

A *New York Herald Tribune* news report, written during the birth of India as a nation-state in 1947, expressed a sanguine hope about the future of India, and had the foresight to see the importance of India's Independence for the world at large.

There seems to be an agreement on substantial progress being made on various fronts in the seventy-five years since Independence. India's agricultural sector has grown by leaps and bounds; she has developed nuclear capabilities and has a thriving technology industry. India is progressing rapidly in space technology that has received further impetus with the historic landing near the Moon's south pole, putting India in an elite club of countries that have achieved a soft landing on the Moon.[2]

India has been successful in making a mark in global politics.[3] India has certainly achieved a lot, considering its history of a long and protracted struggle of more than 200 years through various twists and turns.

Events leading up to Independence were truly a kaleidoscope of crises of enormous proportion, bookended by the end of World War II and the partition of India into two separate independent countries—India and Pakistan.

What is particularly amazing is how India held its spirits high during several crises that arose in the crucial years leading to its Independence, particularly from July 1945 to August 1947. By any yardstick, these two years in the struggle of Independence were tumultuous, to say the least, and several crises were arising at an alarming rate that required someone to step in and work tirelessly to resolve the various issues.

As World War II was coming to an end, India's longstanding demand for self-rule was gaining unprecedented traction with the world powers. Over 180 years of British power was shattered by the long war. At the same time, the US and the Soviet Union emerged as new power centres with great influence. Roosevelt, the US president, particularly supported India's Independence from colonial rule.[4]

However, Winston Churchill, a staunch adversary of Indian Independence, had long argued against self-rule, citing concerns about political chaos and religious strife. He famously said, 'I have not become the King's First Minister in order to preside over the liquidation of the British Empire.'[5]

As luck would have it, Churchill's party lost the election despite winning the war, and there was a change of guard in London when Clement Attlee became Prime Minister on 26 July 1945 after the Labour Party won a landslide victory immediately after the end of the war.[6]

It was, no doubt, a welcome outcome for India's cause. It, nevertheless, threw up new dynamics between Indian leaders and the British government for mapping the broader contours of Independence. The Labour government had a firm desire and plans for keeping India as a dominion under the Crown rather than grant complete independence.[7]

The challenge of Indian leaders for securing independence went a few notches up when the post of the Viceroy (who was the Chief Administrator of India and the representative of the British Crown) became a 'revolving door.' During the crucial period between 1943 and 1947—commonly known as the Fourth

Phase[8]—Indian political leaders had to deal with three Viceroys in quick succession: Lord Linlithgow in 1943, Lord Wavell in 1946 and Lord Mountbatten in late 1946.

The second strand of the crisis was the growing and unbridgeable difference between the Congress and the Muslim League on various issues. The Muslim League had, forcefully, put forward a case for a separate sovereign state of Pakistan comprising Muslim-majority provinces, whereas the Congress continued to work for one united India.[9]

As soon as the Labour government assumed power, it started the process of handing over the powers to Indian leaders in earnest, and sent the Cabinet Mission to India in March 1946 to make it happen. On the eve of the Cabinet Mission's departure for India, Prime Minister Clement Attlee unequivocally declared in Parliament that its sole purpose was to break the seemingly intractable deadlock between the British government and the Indian leaders on the one hand, and the rival political forces of the Congress and the Muslim League on the other (Mosley 1961).

However, the schism between the Congress and the Muslim League had grown so deep that it resulted in the complete failure of the Cabinet Mission Plan.[10]

The failure created a sense of deep helplessness amongst the leaders of the Congress, particularly Nehru and Patel. Accepting the Cabinet Mission Plan proved to be a double-edged sword for Nehru. Though he acquiesced to Gandhi's wishes for the sake of unity, the plan's complex and contentious clauses conflicted with his own ideals of a unified India. When it collapsed, Nehru found himself vulnerable to attacks from those who saw him as either too accommodating or too hesitant, compromising his political standing during a crucial moment in the nation's struggle for Independence (Mosley 1961).

It also frustrated the genuine efforts of the newly elected Labour Prime Minister for granting India's Independence and it shattered the hopes of India getting Independence in the reasonably near future (Mosley 1961).

It ended up forcing Attlee's hand for drawing a timeline for handing over power unilaterally.

On 20 February 1947, Prime Minister Attlee made a declaration in the House of Commons and set a date not later than June 1948 by which Britain would transfer power to responsible Indian hands.[11]

To implement this plan, Attlee appointed a new Viceroy. Viscount Mountbatten of Burma would replace Lord Wavell as Viceroy. As a result, the political leadership in India now had to deal with yet another Viceroy!

Attlee's instructions to Mountbatten were crisp and clear: 'Keep India united if you can. If not, save something from the wreck. In any case, get Britain out.'[12]

Lord Mountbatten, immediately after arriving in India on 22 March, put everyone on notice and conveyed the British Government's resolve to transfer power by June 1948. He was categorical that a solution had to be found within a few months' time (V P Menon 1955).

The departure of Wavell and arrival of Mountbatten presented itself as the final piece of the crisis. By 1947, Indian freedom had become not so much a battle between Britain and India, but between Indian (Congress) and Indian (Muslim League), with the Britishers becoming the referee (Mosley 1961).

THE PROLONGED and tiring struggle for freedom was clearly beginning to take a toll on the leaders who had led India's freedom struggle for many years. The failure of the Cabinet Commission, in particular, brought in a sense of desolation amongst the leaders, who felt they were so near yet so far and were beginning to see new challenges and obstacles that still lay ahead of them (Mosley 1961).

The rapidly shifting sands of polity added to the sense of fatigue and despair amongst the leaders of the freedom movement. It was a reality that none of them knew exactly how to proceed towards the ultimate goal of complete independence.

Fortunately for India, there was a man who happened to be part of the British system for a long time, and he had a firm commitment and conviction towards securing India's independence. He was a true 'sherpa'—dedicated to the cause with the ability to deal with these various crises with clear-headedness and adept resourcefulness.

It was Vappala Pangunni Menon.

VP (as he was fondly known) provided much-needed continuity through the critical period, and played a most crucial role in the unfolding drama of India's Independence.

Unlike his politically active contemporaries who often hailed from elite, British-educated backgrounds, he never studied in England, nor was he a lawyer (Mosley 1961).

He was born in a small village in Kerala in 1893 as the son of a school headmaster. He was part of a large family—a dozen brothers. As a result, he had a poor upbringing with limited resources.[13]

However, VP showed aspirations of carving out a better life for himself, and worked his way to Shimla, where his association with the British establishment began. He diligently worked in various capacities and ultimately became Deputy to Sir Hawthorne Lewis, the Reforms Commissioner, in 1936. VP's capability and skilfulness could be assessed by the fact that

Viceroy Lord Linlithgow appointed him to the post of Reforms Commissioner in 1942. VP thus became the highest serving Indian officer in the Indian Government Service.[14]

VP's knowledge and working style was so profound that when Wavell replaced Linlithgow as Viceroy, VP not only continued as commissioner, but also accompanied him to London on various crucial trips. Although Wavell's term was short, he nevertheless promoted VP to Secretary to the Governor-General (Public) and later to Secretary to the Cabinet.

His career growth since 1936 was meteoric by any yardstick and provided him with unique opportunities to understand the working style of the British. It came in handy when he found himself to be the 'sherpa' for the last three years of India's independence struggle.

VP knew how to perform under pressure and go around a problem to come up with contingency plans and solutions.[15] However, it is a fact that events never go as planned and expected and the real mental fortitude of a sherpa comes to the forefront in this difficult circumstance.

VP's burning ambition for India's independence dimmed under Mountbatten's icy aloofness. He found himself cast as an outsider, the solitary brown face amidst a sea of khaki and tweed, ostracised by the very Viceroy who promised progress. Each morning, as the aroma of breakfast lingered in the air, the hushed murmurs of the 'inner circle' mocked his exclusion—a daily ritual that was chipping away at his resolve to be part of Mountbatten's team (Mosley 1961).

Mountbatten and his core group were in a tearing hurry for 'wrapping up' the process of granting Independence and came out with a 'Dickie Bird Plan.' Mountbatten sent his chief of staff to London for endorsement of the proposed plan.

The Dickie Bird Plan had a 'nasty sting in the tail.' The proposal gave the provinces the right to determine their own future. It allowed the provinces independence initially, and they would subsequently then decide whether to join India, Pakistan or be independent. By any yardstick, this proposal was clearly a death knell to the idea of a unified India!

Nehru did not support the Dickie Bird Plan and said it will lead to the 'balkanisation' of the country. The proposed plan was going against everything that Congress stood for.[16]

Indian freedom leaders such as Nehru knew they did not want the Dickie Bird Plan, but more importantly, they did not know what they wanted, perhaps because they had been close to the issue for far too long. At the same time, Mountbatten himself was beginning to have misgivings about the success of his plan, and had doubts whether Attlee would support it.

One person who knew all along how the whole process would work, and what was required to be done, was the sherpa—VP.

THE JOURNEY of Independence entered a pivotal phase when Mountbatten decided to go to Shimla on 6 May 1947. With his key British advisors in London presenting the Dickie Bird Plan, Mountbatten took the remaining member—VP—to Shimla.

It was a godsent opportunity for VP, who got his first opportunity to talk to Mountbatten freely and openly. All previous interactions were in the presence of four other inner circle members (Mosley 1961).

Like a dedicated sherpa, VP used the opportunity to present his idea of how the future arrangements should and would work between India, Pakistan and Britain. He started the meeting with Mountbatten by saying why the Dickie Bird Plan that was being presented then in London would not work (Mosley 1961).

When he started describing his plan to Mountbatten, he gave the impression that he had thought about it from all potential angles, and knew all the steps required to achieve independence.

During the discussion, VP told how he had laid the groundwork for approval by the Congress by discussing it with Sardar Patel as far back as December 1946.

Mountbatten was certainly interested because, by this time, his original plan in London was facing some challenges. Mountbatten had no choice but to ask VP to produce a plan.

It was VP who had come out with an excellent plan as far back as 1941 that could work as to how the princely states would be assembled within an Independent India well before Sardar Patel swung into action (Mosley 1961).

VP rehashed his own 1941 plan as to how India would remain an essential unity. Mountbatten embraced it. Patel and Nehru were happy too.

'The Menon Plan, at this stage, became the Mountbatten plan.'[17]

When Mountbatten went to London to present the new plan, he had only two people with him—his wife, Lady Mountbatten, and VP!

ALL OF a sudden, the stars aligned for Independence. Congress accepted the Menon Plan and so did the Muslim League. In London, the Labour government accepted the plan and even Winston Churchill and the Conservative (opposition) party approved it (Mosley 1961).

When Mountbatten announced at a press conference on 4 June 1947, that transfer of power would actually happen on 15 August 1947, everyone including Attlee was shocked.

It was now certain India would be a free country on 15 August 1947!

ONCE THE dust of the epic political events started to settle, the leaders were beginning to face one of the main consequences of the Partition. The question was the future of the princely states. There were more than 565 states of varying size and importance, ranging from as large as the size of a typical European country, to a landlord controlling a few thousand acres. These princely states comprised nearly a third of the Indian sub-continent by area and contained a quarter of its population.

VP had a real and accurate assessment of the challenge when he wrote that the 'acceptance of the plan for Independence by everyone involved was one thing, but its implementation was another matter' (Mosley 1961).

Over nearly 200 years, a symbiotic relationship had evolved between the princely states and the British Empire, and clearly these states were reluctant to embrace an unknown situation after Independence.

What made it even more challenging was that the British government decided that paramountcy, together with all treaties between them and the princely states, would come to an end upon the British departure from India. Clearly, Nehru and Patel were anxious and concerned as to how these princely states could be persuaded to sign an agreement on 15 August 1947 to come under the supervision of the new Indian government in New Delhi.[18]

The issue was further complicated, thanks mainly to the Machiavellian manoeuvring by Sir Conrad Laurence Corfield, political advisor to the Viceroy. He was the last official head of the Indian Political Service, which had, for the best part of 100 years, advised, organised, encouraged, cajoled, manipulated and guided the princely states right through the British rule.

Corfield was concerned about the rights of the princes in Independent India. He asserted that the princely states should be allowed to remain independent if they chose to do so. He worked tirelessly, mainly with larger princely states including Hyderabad, to foil India's plan of consolidating the more than 565 princely states within one country.

Again, it was VP the 'sherpa' who was more than a match for Sir Corfield.

As soon as the Congress Party formed a States Ministry with Sardar Patel as the minister, Patel invited VP to be the secretary. However, VP told Patel about his plans to retire after 15 August 1947. Patel invoked a 'sense of duty' by telling VP that at this crucial juncture, people like him should not entertain retirement. VP accepted to be the Sherpa again (Mosley 1961).

This is a fine example of how a political leader must be able to identify a selfless person who has the capacity for the job and support him to lead a "pivotal initiative". This is an important lesson for Amrit Kaal.

Once VP agreed, Patel shared his gravest concern about the short timeframe available for convincing the princely states to join India. However, VP saw an opportunity in the tight timeframe. Clearly, he was a contrarian and took advantage of the situation.

Firstly, VP suggested to Nehru and Sardar Patel that Mountbatten should give an assurance that Britain would oppose the idea of the princely states becoming independent and instead persuade them to join either of the two new nation-states.[19]

To outfox Corfield, VP came up with a plan to approach the princely states with a proposal to accede to the Indian

Union under three subjects only: defence, external affairs and communications.[20] The farsightedness of VP could be seen from the non-confrontational proposal that he gave to the princely states for their accession to India.

The smart proposal for accession was cleverly supported by a carrot-and-stick plan for the rulers of the princely states. VP's 'carrot' part of the proposal included two attractive components—either a privy purse or a pension as compensation, and the authority to retain their palaces and titles.

Most states were ready to accept it. But a few hard-nut-to-crack states were dealt with by the 'stick'. VP and Patel used arm-twisting and veiled threats to pull off the impossible.

Having been in charge of India's transfer of power, his new task was integration. VP drafted what became the Instrument of Accession.

All but three of the 565 princely states signed Instruments of Accession and Standstill Agreements with the forthcoming Indian Union by August 14, 1947.[21]

While Sardar Patel established the framework for integrating the princely states, VP Menon tirelessly executed it through masterful negotiation and diplomacy.

This was the first step towards creating a nation-state.

Over two years, more than 565 princely states were dissolved into 14 new states—a remarkable feat. During this period, Sardar Patel's health had deteriorated significantly, and it was VP who undertook the arduous travel across the length and breadth of the country to meet the princely sates and get their accession in order.

Historians Collins and Lapierre highlight this extent of Menon's work and influence in their book *Freedom at Midnight*.

'What followed was probably the most meteoric rise in that administration's history. By 1947, Menon rose to one of the seniormost posts on the Viceroy's staff, where he had quickly won Mountbatten's confidence and later affection.

No wonder Mountbatten wrote to VP that 'it was a good fortune that you were the reform commissioner on my staff and you found the solution that I never thought of.'

'History must always rate that decision very high, and I owe it to your advice—advice given in the teeth of considerable opposition from other advisors.'

Bureaucrat, crisis manager, handyman and draftsman of India's integration—Menon was all this and more, says Narayani Basu, a historian, foreign policy analyst and VP's great-granddaughter, who has written a well-received biography of VP. She says, 'Being in rooms with different personalities and big egos taught him about drafting sentences and how to negotiate. He learnt, absorbed and adapted.'

VP's honesty for the cause of India's Independence, his working style of thinking about long-term consequences from various angles and his approach of 'biding his time for the opportune moment' for presenting his proposal make a fine example of how the 'designated sherpa' should work during the Amrit Kaal initiative.

INDIA THROUGHOUT its existence was never a geographical, demographic, or culturally unified country before August 1947. As a result, many like Winston Churchill had predicted that post-Independence, India would disintegrate and fall back into the Middle Ages.[22]

India was able to unify into a democracy, and every government since then has taken several steps to make people like Churchill eat their words.

It is truly a stellar achievement.

The unification of India received a shot in the arm through the drafting of a unique and farsighted Constitution that became effective on 26 January 1950, by which India became a republic. The Indian Constitution gave states equal rights in the union. It helped promote national unity by providing a framework for cooperation and coordination between the different levels of government.

This framework has helped India remain a unified country despite its diversity and size.

The next step was taken by the States Reorganisation Act, 1956. It was a major reform of the boundaries of India's states and territories that supported the pivotal initiative. The country was organised into 14 states and six union territories. It remains the single largest reorganisation in the nation's history.

The strength of the union of states was the fact that it was done along linguistic lines, thus keeping the individuality of people/states safeguarded. There was genuine fear, expressed by none other than Viceroy Wavell in 1946, when he said that India will break into linguistic states (Mosley 1961).

This act proved a master-stroke for keeping India together as a nation-state.

Unlike other nations that became independent around the same time, India decided not to impose any one language as a national language. This is in spite of the fact that 66 per cent of the population, living in 70 per cent of the land mass, spoke Hindi. Contrast this with Indonesia, which became independent in 1945 and decided to declare Bahasa as its national language, despite it being the native language of only about 5 per cent of the population.

Allowing different states to continue with their languages contributed to keeping the country together.

The current government has implemented a new initiative to strengthen the unity of the country. The *Ek Bharat Shreshtha Bharat* initiative started on 31 October 2015 with the single objective of increasing the understanding and appreciation of the culture, traditions and practices of different states and Union Territories. It is expected to enhance understanding and bonding between the states, thereby strengthening the unity and integrity of India.[23]

More recently, the New Education Policy announced in 2020 has encouraged the medium of instruction until at least Grade 5 (but preferably until Grade 8 and beyond) in the mother tongue, local language, or regional language.[24] This deliberate thrust will help strengthen the country as a unified entity.

India is a unique and complex country. It is home to a wide variety of religions, castes and languages, which have shaped its culture and society in a profound way. Indians speak a large number of different languages. This linguistic diversity has made it difficult to build a national identity in India, and it has also led to a number of political and social challenges. Despite these challenges, India has remained a vibrant and dynamic country with a rich history and culture before and after 15 August 1947.

Creating a 'united states of India' in 1947 turned out to be as hard as the United States of America! Fortunately, in the case of India, it did not take 172 years for all 50 states to be added to the Union. It was largely due to VP's foresight and doggedness.

India @75 years is not only a testament to the efforts of VP, Sardar Patel and others, but it is also a testament to executing a pivotal initiative of merging more than 565 princely states into a nation-state and to subsequently strengthen it through various policies and other initiatives by successive governments.

***

Rebuilding India without a 'Marshall Plan'

Establishing the Indian Institutes of Technology

'IIT is a world treasure.'

—**Bill Gates at the Flint Center**
Cupertino, CA in 2003

Gates went on to thank the Indian Institutes of Technology in India and the contributions its engineers have made to Microsoft, the company he founded in 1975, in the course of the same speech.

Microsoft has partnered with several IITs in India to empower startups and in the field of cloud computing.

'IIT IS A world treasure,' Bill Gates said while delivering the keynote speech at the 50th anniversary celebration of the founding of the Indian Institute of Technology (IIT) at the Flint Center, Cupertino, CA in 2003. He recognised the contribution that engineers from IIT have made to his company. 'IIT, thank you, bless you.'[1]

Bill Gates' keynote speech, indeed, is a testimony to those who understood the urgency for a pivotal initiative for establishing centres of excellence and higher learning in India at the time when Independence was not even in clear sight. This is a shining example of what can be and must be done during 'Amrit Kaal' to deliver on the promise of a better future for all.

THE FOURTH Phase (1943–1947) of India's freedom struggle was extremely intense and fast-paced, with several crises developing and changing form at the same time.[2] The failure of the Cabinet Mission, the demand from the Muslim League for an independent state, and devising a workable plan for the integration of the princely states, kept the political leadership worried and enormously busy.

The plan for rebuilding of Europe—post-WWII—was well underway as early as 5 June 1947, when the US Secretary of State, George Marshall, proposed a plan with significant United States economic assistance. India, on the other hand, did not feature on the radar of international leaders,[3] even though India's situation was equally dire.

Under British colonisation—for over 200 years—the exploitation of India had been deep and across the board. It is widely reported that the deindustrialisation of India during the eighteenth and nineteenth centuries led to significant loss of GDP (Tharoor 2016). But what has not been well-documented and reported is how it crippled India's higher education, particularly engineering and scientific studies and research.

The intention of British colonial power for higher education in India was clear as day as far back as 1792–93. Their plans and actions for not promoting higher education in line with Europe and the US was based on the loss of the US in 1776. In fact, in a debate in the House of Commons, one of the directors was reported to have observed that 'they had just lost America from their folly in having allowed the establishment of schools and colleges and it would not do for them to repeat the same act of folly in regard to India' (Report of the University Education Commission, 1962).

The East India Company, therefore, focused on improving knowledge of the English language, as it was to become the language of public discourse and of business. This way, one could ensure that Indians served as effective employees and avoid focusing on building universities for Indian students (Report of the University Education Commission, 1962).

In 1811, Lord Minto expressed regret for the neglect of literature and science education in India. However, a measly sum of less than one lakh of rupees in each year was promised to be set aside for the revival and improvement of literature and promotion of knowledge of the sciences among the inhabitants of the British territories in India (Report of the University Education Commission, 1962). Unfortunately, it was just an empty promise, leading nowhere.

By the middle of the nineteenth century, the demand for

trained technicians surfaced, as the colonial power started large-scale public works with the intention of extracting and exporting the natural resources from India. It necessitated the establishment of the first engineering college—Thomason College (now IIT Roorkee), founded in 1847. It was followed by a few more engineering and science universities.

Nevertheless, it was a case of 'too little too late,' as the number of engineering colleges and polytechnics were merely 43 and 44 respectively, with an annual intake capacity of 3,200 and 3,400 students respectively, at the time of Independence in 1947.[4]

THE CRISIS FOR rebuilding India following Independence was deeper and grimmer than that of post-war Europe, particularly in absence of a 'Marshall Plan' for India.

The scale of the crisis was colossal, given what Shashi Tharoor, a Member of Indian Parliament and a prolific writer, wrote in his 2016 book *An Era of Darkness*: '... After 200 years of exploitation, expropriation and clean outright looting, this country was reduced to one of the poorest countries in the world by the time the British left in 1947.'[5]

It was a challenge in light of the paucity of skilled and trained manpower for the decision-makers to help lift the living standards of India's citizens (who constituted one-seventh of the world's population in 1947).[6]

A TURN of events around 1945 squeezed the political leaders from all directions, particularly the failure of the Cabinet Mission, which forced the hands of the political leadership to squarely focus on achieving Independence. They didn't have the capacity to plan how India, as an independent country, would go about building infrastructure, including new roads and railways, let alone establish new industrial powerhouses and conduct scientific research for improving the lives of its citizens.

Fortunately, some work had been done in 1943 when the Nobel Laureate Professor A V Hill was invited to map out steps for higher education in engineering and scientific research, as a part of India's post-war reconstruction plan.[7]

Professor Hill visited India for almost five months—from 16 November 1943 to 5 April 1944—and travelled through most parts of the country. He submitted a detailed report titled 'A Report to the Government of India on Scientific Research in India'.[8]

It was a comprehensive report and could serve as a benchmark—even today—for its analysis of the problems in education and research that India faced leading up to Independence. Professor Hill identified that the expansion of research in India should be exclusively funded by the government and that directing scientific research through a central organisation was better for coordination, so that a common plan could be evolved in the best interests of the country. A single central organisation, which would function under the Member (Minister) for Planning and Development, was suggested.

Medicine and public health, agriculture and animal husbandry, industry, surveys and industrial resources and engineering were identified as focus areas. Liaison between India and other prosperous countries was recommended for reducing the time required to build skill sets.[9]

WITH THIS backdrop, a motley crew of three individuals took it upon themselves to map a pivotal initiative for establishing institutes of higher learning in line with Professor Hill's recommendations. These 'sherpas' neither waited for the political leadership to provide guidance nor for India to become a free nation. They embarked upon defining the contours of the pivotal initiative in earnest.

It is particularly impressive that the entire process of conceptualisation and establishment of centres of excellence and higher learning in India, was designed and worked on by individuals, not by a politician, even before India was a free nation. These individuals, from diverse backgrounds, ensured that all aspects of this arduous task were debated and discussed extensively. Some of the topics considered included comprehensive budgets, assessing the complementarity of each centre with others, geographical locations and the courses that would be offered to students. What is even more amazing, is that this was all done in a record time of less than two years.

The three gentlemen were Sir Nalini Ranjan Sarkar, Sir Jogendra Singh and Sir Ardeshir Dalal. Each one of them had successively served as members of the Viceroy's Executive Council, and as a result, all of them had influence in the decision making.

Sir Sarkar served in the council between 1941 and 1943, followed by Sir Singh from July 1942 to 1946 and finally Sir Dalal from June 1944 to January 1946.[10]

Each of these members was an accomplished individual in their own right. Sir Sarkar was president of the Federation of Indian Chambers of Commerce & Industry in 1933. Sir Ardeshir Dalal was an Indian Civil Service officer-turned-Tata Steel executive. Sir Jogendra Singh was an editor, author and former prime minister of Patiala, who also introduced mechanised farming to Punjab. Between them, they perhaps covered all industries and possessed a deep understanding of how the US had built industries and its network of roadways and highways.

Sir Ardeshir Dalal's responsibilities within the Executive Council included drawing up a comprehensive plan for the post-war reconstruction of India. He immediately realised the scale of the trained manpower crisis when he leant there were only 36 institutions for first-degree engineering education, with an annual intake of as little as 2,500 students.[11]

His original idea was initially focused on persuading the US government to offer doctoral fellowships to Indian scientists, so that they came back qualified enough to lead the newly established Council for Scientific and Industrial Research (CSIR).

However, he soon realised that this arrangement with the US government could only be a short-term solution and that the emerging new India needed institutions that would become nurseries for qualified scientific and technical manpower.[12]

He foresaw that the future prosperity of India would depend on technology.

As a result, he quickly worked up a plan for institutes within India that would train such workforces in the country itself. This is considered to be the first conceptualisation of the Indian Institutes of Technology (IITs).[13]

Emerging from the challenges of post-colonial India, these institutions envisioned themselves as catalysts for national development, training generations of scientists and engineers who would drive economic growth and societal advancement after 1947.[14]

ONE OF the key learnings from this pivotal initiative for Amrit Kaal is how the change of guards in the Viceroy Executive Council did not derail the process of establishing these institutes of excellence. In fact, each successive member relied on the preceding member for pushing the initiative and appointed the preceding member for a pivotal role in the subsequent efforts. The objectives of establishing centres of higher learning remained constant over time, even in the din of political changes.

However, the political turmoil affected every facet of life at that time, and Sir Sarkar resigned from the council in the wake of Mahatma Gandhi's imprisonment in 1942. But the vision of the pivotal initiative was not derailed.

As soon as Sir Jogendra Singh succeeded Sir Sarkar as the Member for Health, Lands and Education, he constituted a twenty-two-member committee that was entrusted with the main objective of preparing detailed plans for establishing 'Higher Technical Institutions' to drive the post-war industrial development in India.

Sir Singh took a smart step for assuring the continuation of the project by making Sir N R Sarkar the head of this committee, and it proved a masterstroke for implementing the pivotal initiative.

During the consultation process, the committee was clearly aware of Professor Hill's report. They made use of it by aiming high—to establish institutes of excellence similar to the Ivy League in the US.[15]

In a short timeframe, the official committee headed by N R Sarkar submitted a report on the development of higher technical institutions to the government (Sarkar Interim Report of the Committee, 1946).

A 'deep dive' into this report shows what an astonishing achievement indeed it was! It can serve as a blueprint for new pivotal initiatives during Amrit Kaal showing how a 360-degree analysis of issues is required for every new initiative.

For starters, the committee decided to submit an interim

report in line with the urgency of the matter, following the '80:20 rule,' rather than optimising all aspects of the report.

The committee rightly identified the challenge of securing the services of the right type of engineers, architects, technologists and planners from Europe and the US, due to the calls of reconstruction in Europe on account of the Marshall Plan. The report highlighted the urgency for the initiation of a programme of higher technical education and research in India with the utmost speed and determination.

The report recommended establishing a central institution (possibly along the lines of the Massachusetts Institute of Technology), with a number of subordinate institutions affiliated to it. In addition, several regional higher learning centres were recommended.

The report also outlined in detail the scope and size of the proposed institution or institutions and their geographical locations, along with an ideal control and management of the institutions. In addition, it defined the qualifications and conditions of service of the teachers to be employed therein, and mapped out the best way of recruiting them.

It appears that all twenty-two members worked extensively to the limit of exhaustion. The comprehensive nature of the report included detailed specifications for an excellence centre, including buildings and even the equipment it would require with a breakdown of the potential cost.

The clarity of their thinking can be seen from the fact that the committee strongly recommended no less than four Higher Technical Institutions, one each in the north, east, south and west, for satisfying the post-war requirements.

Interestingly, there was no 'political compulsion' for satisfying a political constituency, as is the case nowadays worldwide, including in my home country, Australia. The recommendation was purely based on on-the-ground realities and leveraging existing strengths.

What is really astonishing is that the committee worked out a complementarity between the proposed centres, keeping in mind the size of the country and the location of India's industries in the mid-1940s. There was a clear intent to create a provision of several higher technical institutions, so that it could satisfy post-war requirements.

The committee made detailed recommendations about the scope and size of the proposed institutions. To meet post-war manpower requirements, all the institutes were to of course provide undergraduate instruction in the main branches of technology (civil, electrical, mechanical). Other branches to be taught at each institute were to be decided according to regional needs—for instance, metallurgy and chemical engineering in Calcutta and Bombay, textile engineering and naval architecture in Bombay, hydraulics in Kanpur and so on.[16]

The committee provided further evidence of the manpower crisis by stressing the need to maintain a close-knit relationship between the public, industry and education. The committee's final recommendation was to build the proposed institutions in such locations throughout the country that, once built, they would be within easy reach of large industrial areas.

That's the reason why the northern institution centre was proposed to be established in Kanpur as an engineering nucleus—to cater to the need for engineers (in particular, of the Central Public Works Department for civil engineers) with specialised knowledge in hydraulics.

Interestingly, there was an excellent understanding of the required expertise of each institute to be built. Whilst the western and eastern centres were to offer degrees in geology, geophysics and mining engineering, these courses were not included in Kanpur and Delhi.

Immediately after Independence, the new 'sherpas' swung into action in the process of executing the initiative. These were influential people from Bengal and pursued the task of establishing the first Institute of Technology in line with the comprehensive report of Sir Sarkar.

The rationale for setting up the first institute in West Bengal was because this state then had the highest concentration of engineering students.

The planning was done under the guidance of Sir J C Ghosh, the then director of the Indian Institute of Science (IISc), Bangalore, with the help of two bureaucrats posted at the Education Ministry—L S Chandrakant and Biman Sen.[17]

The Education Secretary, Humayun Kabir (who later became chairman of the University Grants Commission), persuaded Dr Bidhan Chandra Roy, West Bengal's second Chief Minister, to set up the first Indian Institute of Technology in his state, and try and find appropriate land to establish it. Roy took his advice seriously and found the Hijli Detention Camp at Kharagpur as an appropriate site. This camp notoriously housed several Bengali freedom fighters that had been imprisoned during the struggle for Independence.

Initially the Institute started functioning from 5 Esplanade East, Calcutta (now Kolkata), and shifted to Hijli in September 1950.

The present name, 'Indian Institute of Technology,' was adopted before the formal inauguration of the Institute on 18 August 1951, by Maulana Abul Kalam Azad, India's then Education Minister.

This was the first time a politician had become part of the pivotal initiative—a remarkable fact given how much progress had already been made.

In the first convocation address of IIT Kharagpur in 1956, Jawaharlal Nehru, India's first Prime Minister, said, 'Here in the place of that Hijli Detention Camp stands the fine monument of India, representing India's urges, India's future in the making. This picture seems to me symbolical of the changes that are coming to India.'[18]

WITH THE first IIT established, there was demand from other states for establishing other IITs in line with the initiative.

As a result, the political leadership swung into action and approached international agencies and friendly countries for assistance. In 1956, IIT Bombay became the second institute of excellence. UNESCO provided cooperation and participation, but it was the erstwhile USSR or Soviet Union that gave the necessary assistance in the form of equipment and expert services through UNESCO from 1956 to 1973. IIT received 59 experts and 14 technicians from several reputed institutions in the USSR. UNESCO also offered 27 fellowships for training Indian faculty members. Under the bilateral agreement of 1965, the Government of USSR provided additional assistance to supplement the aid programme already received by the Institute through UNESCO.

Established in 1958, IIT Bombay (IITB) was the first to be set up with foreign assistance. The funds from UNESCO came as rubles from the then Soviet Union. Since then, IITB has grown from strength to strength and emerged as one of the top technical universities in the world.[19]

In 1956, Pandit Jawaharlal Nehru went on an official visit to West Germany. The Federal Republic of Germany offered assistance in setting up a higher technological institute in India. This resulted in the signing of the first Indo-German Agreement in Bonn in 1958 for the establishment of an IIT at Madras.

The Indo-German agreements provided for the services of German professors and foremen, training facilities for Indian faculty members and the supply of scientific and technical equipment for the establishment of the central workshop and laboratories at IIT Madras.

During this period, the Cold War between the USSR and the US was at its peak. Global geopolitics left their mark on higher education in India as well when, following the Soviet Union's involvement in IITB, the Americans offered to help set up an IIT in the north. This led to the establishment of IIT Kanpur in Uttar Pradesh in 1959.[20]

Though IIT Kanpur was said to cater to northern India, the Chief Engineer of Chandigarh, R N Dogra, argued that Uttar Pradesh was part of Central India. He persuaded the Planning Commission to set up an IIT in Delhi.

As a result, IIT Delhi, with an area of 320 acres, arose in 1961 and was built with the help of the UK Government. The Indian Institutes of Technology Act was accordingly amended to include the additional IITs. Dogra himself was appointed as the first director of IIT Delhi.[21]

With five premier IITs established by 1961, the main thrust of this pivotal initiative was completed with great satisfaction.

Then the next logical step was a Parliament Act covering the initiative, and on 19 December 1961, the Institute of Technology Act 1961 received the assent of the President of India. Under this act, these institutions of technology became institutions of national importance.

The current President, Droupadi Murmu, didn't exaggerate when she said, while speaking at the closing ceremony of the Diamond Jubilee celebrations of IIT Delhi, that the IITs proved to the world the capability of India in the domains of education and technology. In more than one way, the story of the IITs is the story of independent India. The IITs have contributed immensely to India's improved standing on the global stage today. The faculty and alumni of IITs have shown the world our brainpower. Some of those who studied in IIT Delhi and in other IITs are now at the forefront of the digital revolution sweeping the world. Moreover, the impact of IITs has gone beyond science and technology. 'IITians' are leaders in every walk of life—in education, industry, entrepreneurship, civil society, activism, journalism, literature and politics.[22]

THE WARS with Pakistan and China have had a profound impact. They led to a loss of confidence in the government and a sense of vulnerability in the country. The state of emergency declared in 1975 further eroded public trust in the government and led to a period of political instability.

The net result was that successive governments lost the drive for establishing new centres of excellence, including new IITs, and no new IITs were established in India after 1963. India lost momentum for training its young in line with international standards.

After a long gap of 30 years, the sixth IIT was established in Guwahati in the state of Assam. What was even more disappointing, was that the proposal to set this up was a result of political pressure from the Assam agitation rather than the need for a new centre of excellence.

In August 2018, addressing the 56th annual convocation of IITB, India's Prime Minister, Mr Modi said IIT graduates were at the forefront of some of the best startups in the country.

'These are the startups which are also at the forefront of solving so many national problems,' Modi had said.[23]

THE CURRENT government, when elected in 2014—started implementing the initiative with renewed vigour and approved the establishment of six new IITs in 2015.

The growth of the pivotal initiative received a shot in the arm in 2023 when the current government started the internationalisation of IITs with the idea of setting up branches in other countries. The Indian Institute of Technology Madras (IITM) has become the first IIT in the country to set up a campus outside India, opening in Zanzibar, Tanzania, in October 2023.[24]

Indian Institute of Technology Delhi has just opened a new campus in Abu Dhabi in September 2024. Also, IIT Kharagpur is working on opening a campus in Kuala Lumpur, Malaysia.[25,26]

WITHOUT QUESTION, the IITs are the crown jewels of Indian higher education. They are world-renowned for the quality of their graduates, for their academic programmes in a range of technology and engineering fields and in the past decade, for their research and innovation through research parks. They are among the few Indian higher education institutions that find a place in global rankings.

The sherpas—Dalal, Sarkar, Singh—as well as the countless others that helped along the way, would be proud of the impact that the IITs have made on the world stage today.

Indeed, it was a pivotal initiative well worth their efforts.

***

From 'Begging Bowl' to 'Breadbasket'
Green Revolution

The Green Revolution has an entirely different meaning to most people in the affluent nations of the privileged world than to those in the developing nations of the forgotten world.

—Norman Borlaug

If agriculture goes wrong, nothing else will have a chance to go right.

—M S Swaminathan

INDIA'S SECOND Prime Minister, Lal Bahadur Shastri's 'miss-a-meal-once-a-week' clarion call to his countrymen in 1964[1] was not part of a solution for the food grain crisis of monumental proportions in India at the time, but a sign of sheer desperation!

India's journey as a free nation wasn't a smooth one. In August 1947, India was a free nation, but it was a hungry nation. When the transfer of power from the British happened, India had a starving and malnourished populace.[2]

A rather messy partition of India into two independent countries led to bloodshed and the loss of lives of humongous proportions. At least 14 million people were displaced and as many as one million were killed in the violence.[3] The humanitarian crisis was so large that the new government had to work overtime to rehabilitate displaced families, particularly in light of the monsoon flooding. Several refugee camps were established across the Indian sub-continent, with the largest emerging in Lahore and Delhi.

The partition also resulted in the loss of a large part of fertile land to Pakistan (both West Pakistan and East Pakistan, now Bangladesh), and it had a far bigger consequence than felt at that time. The loss of prime agricultural land with a widespread irrigation system was one the major reasons India lived as a starving nation right through the 1950s and 1960s.[4]

But there were several policy missteps that contributed to the severe food crisis in the country.

To start with, the government in the 1950s adopted a rather unique strategy of economic development with a strong focus on rapid industrialisation by implementing centrally prepared five-year plans via large industrial state-owned enterprises (SOEs).[5] However, these plans came at the sacrifice of other resources. The net result of this strategy was that the first two five-year plans (between 1951 and 1961) couldn't allocate sufficient budget for increasing the food production capacity of the country.

Many international experts, perhaps, had a better sense of the crisis and were nudging Indian politicians and decision makers to focus on agriculture as a priority as early as 1950.[6]

Right through the 1950s and early 1960s, US-based private foundations and philanthropic institutes, as well as the US government, made genuine efforts to improve agriculture output in India by engaging with the Indian government at various levels. The Rockefeller Foundation sent an expert team consisting of Warren Weaver, J George Harrar and Paul C Mangelsdorf to India in 1951 to study the farming practices in India. They compiled their findings in detail as a discussion paper titled 'Notes on Indian Agriculture.' As a newly independent and democratic country, India offered a potential area of expansion for the agricultural initiatives of the Rockefeller Foundation, as opposed to the communist countries of greater Asia at that time.[7]

However, the Rockefeller Foundation soon realised that there was a complete lack of existing infrastructure for agriculture in India. Their main concerns were the lack of large areas for crop plantation, the limited irrigation network and the lack of fertiliser. As a result, it compelled the Rockefeller Foundation to proceed cautiously.

The Indian government kicked the issue into the proverbial long grass and preferred to import grains from the US under the Agricultural Trade Development and Assistance Act (PL 480) from 1954. Over time, India became the largest participant of the PL 480 programme. The import of grain wasn't addressing the main issue, but a few influential politicians within the government believed and argued publicly that it was cheaper to import food grains than to incentivise domestic agricultural production.[8]

THE ALARM bells started to ring louder in 1957–58 when food production fell to a five-year low of 62 million tonnes. It highlighted the miserable state of Indian agriculture. Around the same time, the then Prime Minister Jawaharlal Nehru was strongly urged by a team of US experts to restore primacy to agriculture over industry in the second five-year plan.[9]

To make thing worse, India was engaged in two wars—in 1962 with China and in 1965 with Pakistan. As a result, a large part of the budget was diverted towards defence procurement and preparedness. The agriculture budget received 'step-brotherly treatment' yet again during the next five-year plan (1961–66).

At the same time, the population of the country had started to grow rapidly in the early 1960s. As a result, there were more mouths to feed every year—from 353 million in 1947 to 580 million in 1965.[10]

The United Nations' Food and Agriculture Organisation's comprehensive studies of 1961 predicted that in five years, India's population would outstrip the production of rice and wheat and the country would face a major calamity.[11]

Yet policymakers decided to bury their heads in the proverbial sand.

The straw that broke the camel's back was the successive failure of the monsoon in 1964–66. It was, by any yardstick, one of the worst droughts the country had faced in 40 years.[12]

Consequently, India faced a famine-like situation and its government and its bureaucracy were woken up with a jolt.

THE UNFORTUNATE death of Pandit Nehru in May 1964 brought in a new Prime Minister. Lal Bahadur Shastri, perhaps, had less baggage of the past. More importantly, he clearly had full visibility of the graveness of the situation. When Shastri took over as PM, the food grain production growth halved due to three successive failed monsoons. However, it was not just a result of the drought, it was also a result of successive policy failures.[13]

Nevertheless, Shastri was determined to correct course and he rightly thought he needed to assign someone who had the stomach to tackle the issue head-on.

He went with the tried-and-tested approach of offering the position of Agriculture Minister to political stalwarts, with the hope that influential politicians would be able to find a solution to the crisis. To his surprise as well as disappointment, everyone politely declined—perhaps knowing the 'Himalayan' task required for uplifting agricultural output.[14]

Shastri demonstrated unusual political will and courage when he personally approached C Subramaniam, who held the steel and heavy industries portfolio under Nehru, to take charge of the crucial issue of food and agriculture.[15]

It proved a masterstroke, as C Subramaniam brought energy, vigour and decisiveness to a job that had previously been regarded as a political treadmill.[16]

IN THE crucial and desperate year of 1965—right in the middle of the severe drought—C Subramaniam, with unwavering support of his PM, identified various strands of the pivotal initiative that were to be worked on simultaneously for transforming India into a self-sufficient country in grain production.

What was incredible was that he worked on every aspect

of the crisis simultaneously and used every trick possible for working with every stakeholder, right from the President of the US to the naysayers within his own political party in India. The working style and clear-headedness of C Subramaniam, who worked on all aspects of the crises simultaneously rather than sequentially, offers a ready template for designing a pivotal initiative during Amrit Kaal.

C Subramanian was no doubt the political architect of India's Green Revolution.[17]

C Subramaniam immediately came up with a strategy for the initiative that had three interrelated strands: one, to provide price incentives to farmers; two, to encourage farmers to adopt science and technology-based agricultural practices; and finally, to work all his charm in convincing the Johnson administration in the US to continue with the food aid programme for the foreseeable future.

Working with immediacy, he set up the Food Corporation of India (FCI) in July 1964, within three months of taking over the reign of the new ministry.[18] His main aim was to give farmers an attractive price for the grains, so that they felt the incentive to increase production. He nevertheless faced criticism for this initiative due to the increased subsidy, but he went ahead with his PM's support.

Once he found his feet, he decided to take the bull by the horns. On 1 January 1965, in the premium body of the National Development Council, C Subramaniam forcefully argued that the only way to increase food grain production was by wider use of science in reforming Indian agriculture, including the use of better seeds, more and better use of fertilisers and more efficient use of irrigation.

He did not waste any time and reorganised the crucial and

premium body—the Indian Council of Agricultural Research (ICAR) and, for the first time, appointed a scientist, Dr B P Pal as director general. His main mantra to the scientific community of ICAR was to conduct research on high-yielding variety (HYV) seeds. And he regularly interacted with them to check on the progress.

In one such meeting, he found the 'technical sherpa' for his pivotal initiative of increasing food grain production in the country. He noticed a scientist who seemed to be excited about his plans. That person was none other than Dr M S Swaminathan, who was ultimately recognised as the 'father' of India's Green Revolution.[19]

It was Dr Swaminathan who made C Subramaniam aware that new HYVs had been developed by Norman Borlaug's team in Mexico. Dr Swaminathan argued that India must launch large-scale field demonstrations immediately.[20]

C Subramaniam was convinced of Dr Swaminathan's recommendation and immediately ordered 200 tonnes of seed for one variety (Sonora 64) from Borlaug in July 1965, followed by another order of 50 tonnes of the second variety (Lerma Rojo 64A). The main idea was these seeds would be used for testing, demonstrations and distribution to 5,000 farmers.

However, C Subramaniam didn't realise the uphill battle that was awaiting him when the HYV seeds landed at Gujarat's port.

This perhaps is another important lesson for the implementation of a pivotal initiative: challenges would be cropping up with regularity, and the sherpa has to dig deep to find courage, resourcefulness and determination to overcome it and push forward.

There were several naysayers expressing negative views about the HYVs, including nationalists, farmers, farmer unions and political leaders.[21] The critics were concerned about the potential of introducing foreign pests and diseases in Indian fields and native vegetation. Concerns were raised—loudly—about the potential of ruining the already-impoverished Indian farmer. The nationalists had a rather bizarre take when they argued against the reliability of the seeds developed by an American scientist, Norman Borlaug.

C Subramaniam was frustrated with the illogical protest, particularly when the same seeds had achieved significant grain productions in Mexico. He was certain of the science of the seeds, and its necessity for India.

As a first step, he prepared a technical paper on the 'Application of Technology in Agriculture' and circulated it widely among influential cynics. Second, he placed an order for import of 10,000 tonnes of Mexican HYV seeds for wheat cultivation, despite objections from the Finance Ministry.

To convince the naysayers, he even tilled the five-acre garden and the cricket pitch around his ministerial house and sowed the same HYV wheat seeds that he had ordered.[22]

His life within Parliament was not comfortable. The opposition created several roadblocks for introducing the new seed varieties, to the extent that Shastri's short-lived government faced three no-confidence motions on the issue.

Like a true sherpa, he persisted with his efforts, and shifted his gear to focus his efforts on the farmers rather than the naysayers.

In his efforts to convince the farmers, he took unconventional steps. He travelled across the country and personally met farmers to gauge their response, rather than relying on bureaucrats and their reports. He initiated a unique idea of 'farmer's clubs' all over the country and his sincerity and conviction propelled these clubs.[23] The formation of these farmer's clubs marked a pivotal moment in his campaign to win over the hearts and minds of the agricultural community. He employed his formidable skills as a political persuader and administrator to spread the use of a new wheat variety to more than a million Indian farmers.[24]

C Subramaniam and Dr Swaminathan were working overtime on the aspects of the crisis that were within their control and were making significant progress against all odds.

But the 'Rain God' continued to play spoilsport.

1965 turned out to be the worst year for the monsoon. It was the third consecutive year with significantly deficient rainfall. C Subramaniam's struggle was not getting easier. He had unwavering support from his PM and was winning battles against internal opponents, but he had a bigger challenge with policymakers within the US government.

It was obvious that India would yet again have to import a large quality of grain to overcome the crisis.

Prior to C Subramaniam's leadership in agriculture, dealings with Indian politicians had caused some frustration within the US government. A key source of this tension was India's persistent reluctance to significantly increase agricultural spending in its next five-year plan. Additionally, the US government desired a shift in Indian agricultural policies to encourage wider adoption of fertilisers and high-yielding, disease-resistant wheat varieties.

As a consequence, President Johnson, in particular, was hardening his stance and had expressed his views that the Indian government had become complacent, and had started receiving the grain under the PL480 scheme as an entitlement. In frustration, President Johnson started a practice of personally intervening in every food aid decision related to India, even to the extent that during the severe drought period of 1965, the food aid to India was provided only on a month-to-month basis.[25]

Dr Swaminathan later described the crisis that prevailed in India in the mid-1960s: 'During ... that critical period of drought (1965–67), President Johnson, because of certain policies he had adopted, was releasing wheat only in driblets. At one point, we reached a stage where there were stocks for only two weeks and nothing else in the pipeline.'[26]

To effectively guide Amrit Kaal's response to various crises, an early assessment of the situation from all angles is crucial. A key lesson is to design and implement an appropriate pivotal initiative at an appropriate time, rather than when the situation becomes particularly dire.

C Subramaniam sensed the urgency for convincing the US administration for tonnes more of US food grain to help stave off its worst food crisis in two decades. He decided to approach President Johnson personally. Before catching his flight, he had done his homework exceptionally well and had got all his ducks in a row. One month before, in November 1965, he flew to Rome to attend the week-long biannual conference of agricultural ministers, organised by the UN Food and Agriculture Organization. Before going to Rome, he worked with Lester R Brown, who was the direct report to Orville L Freeman, the Secretary of Agriculture in New Delhi. In Rome, he had several meetings with Secretary of Agriculture, Orville L Freeman, sometimes at a private location in the residence of US Ambassador to Italy, Frederick Reinhardt.[27]

At the end of meetings that stretched over a few days, C Subramaniam gave a commitment to Freeman that India will focus on agriculture in a new five-year plan, and the budgetary allocation will be to the tune of $11 billion for fertiliser, farm machinery, irrigation and better seed, with the aim of increasing farm output by nearly 50 per cent by 1971. C Subramaniam, on his return to India from Rome, appraised PM Shastri of the agreement reached in Rome.[28]

He then flew to Washington, just before Christmas of 1965, for talks with President Johnson. President Johnson could clearly see the sincerity in C Subramaniam's body language. He agreed for the release of at least 13 million tonnes of grain.

Johnson interacted with Subramaniam, and later with Indira Gandhi who took over as PM after Shastri's death in Tashkent, over multiple state dinners and parties. He reportedly enjoyed Subramaniam and Gandhi's company, even cancelling or rearranging prior commitments to spend time with Indian delegations.[29]

C Subramaniam was the political father of the Green Revolution in India and was ably supported by Dr Swaminathan, who was the technical father of the Green Revolution and worked as a sherpa in tandem with C Subramaniam.

Dr Swaminathan was at the helm of the scientific community that spearheaded the project with dedication.[30] His team developed new wheat varieties that helped yield higher levels of grain as well as develop stalk structures strong enough to support the increased biomass for Indian conditions.[31]

Like the political father of the Green Revolution, Dr Swaminathan fought his own battle with Indian scientists who opposed the bringing in of the Mexican seeds. The Indian scientists argued that their research was on the verge of a major breakthrough for increasing production of an Indian variety.

Dr Swaminathan and other scientists, taking directions from C Subramaniam, ignored these assertions and conducted several trials under different climatic conditions in India. The trials were a roaring success.

He focused his attention and energy on Indian farmers who were not literate at the time. He designed new methods and guidance to teach Indian farmers how to effectively increase production by employing a combination of HYV wheat, fertilisers and more efficient farming techniques. This proved an important step in India's efforts in solving the food grain crisis.

He came up with the unique idea of demonstrating how to plant the seeds in several test plots in the northern part of the country as soon as the Mexican HYV seeds arrived in India in 1965.

In a pre-digital era, he made films to demonstrate to farmers how to increase production by using different farming techniques by setting up 2,000 model farms in villages outside New Delhi.[32]

This innovative approach overcame the obstacles of illiteracy and lack of formal education. It laid the groundwork for a generation of Indian farmers with knowledge of the effectiveness of modern agriculture.

The ingenuity of C Subramaniam, combined with the scientific prowess of Dr Swaminathan and continued support of political leadership, solved the hunger crisis of India effectively.

The results of their hard work could be seen when, in the first-year harvest, crop yields surged like a triumphant wave, tripling the previous year's meagre harvest.

Another benefit was seen in overall scientific advances, as more and more farmers started using the HYV seeds. India's total crop yield of wheat increased from 12 million tonnes to 23 million tonnes in four crop seasons, which effectively ended India's reliance on grain imports.

USHERING IN the Green Revolution in an impoverished and diverse country with challenging terrain, riddled with political and bureaucratic obstacles through a pivotal initiative, was indeed a remarkable feat.

Two intrepid sherpas, fuelled by their unwavering belief, navigated every crevice and conquered every summit. Their perseverance, not just with the US government but also with their own party and government, paved the way for the Green Revolution's bountiful harvest.

C Subramaniam's vision and dexterity, combined with the scientific prowess of Dr Swaminathan, transformed India from a 'begging bowl' to a 'breadbasket' almost overnight.[33]

It was truly an outstanding achievement against all odds.

SUCCESSIVE GOVERNMENTS implemented policies and new initiatives to boost the achievement of the Green Revolution for sustaining and further increasing grain production. It proved crucial in feeding the ever-increasing population.

One such initiative was the launch of Krishi Darshan, a TV programme on Doordarshan, the national TV channel, on 26 January 1967. This programme disseminated essential knowledge and information on agricultural techniques and practices to the largely illiterate farming community. [34]

Fortunately, Dr Swaminathan continued to guide and spearhead the success of the Green Revolution and remained at the helm of agricultural affairs with the new Prime Minister Indira Gandhi, who succeeded Shastri in government after his untimely death.

He helped establish agricultural policies and programmes that resulted in long-term self-sufficiency across the country.

He designed a four-step strategy. It included strong research and development for new seed varieties, providing price assurances to producers through a robust minimum support price system and maintained a buffer stock and distribution of food grain through an effective public distribution system.[35]

Following the success of the Green Revolution, various states enacted Agricultural Produce Markets Regulation (APMR) Acts during the 1960s and 1970s and brought all primary wholesale markets under their ambit.

New initiatives in the areas of irrigation projects, subsidies on fertilisers and seeds and new research focused on HYVs were implemented.

PM-KISAN, initiated in 2019, is an income support scheme designed to assist small and marginal farmers.

Launched in 2015, the Soil Health Card Scheme provides personalised soil health reports to farmers, offering valuable insights on soil nutrients and recommendations for balanced fertilisation. By promoting proper soil management practices, this scheme has optimised yields, reduced input costs and enhanced soil health across agricultural lands.

Launched in 2015, the Paramparagat Krishi Vikas Yojana scheme promotes organic farming practices and the adoption of traditional and indigenous methods. Through financial support and technical guidance, this scheme encourages farmers to pursue organic farming certification, contributing to sustainable agriculture, improved soil fertility and healthier farming practices.

A STRONG and well-functioning agricultural sector is critical for India's transition to middle-income status. The successful and effective implementation of the Green Revolution pivotal initiative has turned India into a grain-surplus country.

***

'Smiling Buddha' to 'Operation Shakti'

Becoming a Nuclear-Weapon State

Today, at 15:45 hours, India conducted three underground nuclear tests in the Pokhran range. These tests conducted today were with a fission device, a low-yield device, and a thermonuclear device. The measured yields are in line with expected values. Measurements have also confirmed that there was no release of radioactivity into the atmosphere. These were contained explosions like the experiment conducted in May 1974. I warmly congratulate the scientists and engineers who have carried out these successful tests.

—Atal Bihari Vajpayee

Indian Prime Minister, 11 May 1998

It's an unprecedented deal for India … If you look at the three countries outside the Nuclear Non-Proliferation Treaty—Israel, India, and Pakistan—this stands to be a unique deal.

—Charles D Ferguson

Science and technology fellow at the Council on Foreign Relations, 1 October 2008

THE ANNOUNCEMENT on 11 May 1998, by the then Indian Prime Minister about conducting nuclear tests,[1] sent shockwaves around the world. It was a moment of widespread surprise, catching many off guard and raising international concerns about nuclear proliferation in a volatile region.

The euphoria of World War II's conclusion, with the founding of the United Nations aiming for a peaceful future, was shattered by the development of nuclear weapons by the US.[2]

This innovation cast a long, dark shadow, raising anxieties about a potential global catastrophe. The following decades, from 1945 to 1998, were dominated by the Cold War, a tense ideological and geopolitical power struggle between the US and the Soviet Union. However, India's own nuclear programme added a fresh layer of alarm to this already-precarious security landscape, culminating in the decision to conduct nuclear tests in 1998.

Following Independence in 1947, India charted a bold course for its foreign policy, deliberately distancing itself from the traditional power blocs of the Cold War. This independent spirit led them to play a pivotal role in founding the Non-Aligned Movement, advocating neutrality and peaceful coexistence between the superpowers.[3]

However, India's relationship with nuclear weapons has been a source of intrigue. Despite not signing the Nuclear Non-Proliferation Treaty (NPT), India has consistently called for global disarmament efforts. This seemingly contradictory stance has sparked debate on the world stage.

India became a staunch proponent of nuclear disarmament as soon as it became an independent country. India's first prime minister, Jawaharlal Nehru, made several proposals for nuclear disarmament at the United Nations.[4]

However, some critics argue that India's non-aligned approach came at a strategic cost. This was particularly true during the formative years of the nuclear order, between 1947 and 1968, when the NPT was established. A key decision that continues to shape India's strategic calculus was its choice to forgo the NPT. This decision, driven by a desire for strategic autonomy, arguably resulted in a sense of isolation as regional security concerns intensified.[5]

After World War II, with India gaining independence in 1947, the US found itself as the sole nuclear power. This dominance prompted several world leaders, including the Australian Prime Minister, to call for the establishment of an international control system to manage nuclear weapons.

The proposed control system, envisioned to limit the spread of nuclear weapons and ensure compliance with restrictions (such as a ban on fissile material production for bombs), faced a harsh reality check. The successful Soviet atomic bomb test in 1949 shattered this dream. By the early 1960s, the emergence of China, France and the UK as nuclear powers further eroded hopes for control. This rapid nuclear proliferation ignited a multitude of anxieties. The spectre of an uncontrollable arms race, the possibility of accidental detonations and heightened geopolitical tensions loomed large. Even more alarmingly, many other countries seemed determined to join the exclusive club of nuclear powers.[6]

In response, many countries, both independently and through the UN, began working on a proposal for a comprehensive NPT. The treaty was envisioned as the cornerstone of a global nuclear non-proliferation regime, aiming to pave the way for serious pursuit of nuclear disarmament.[7]

India actively participated in efforts towards nuclear disarmament and achieving a comprehensive treaty. Given this, one might expect India to be an early signatory to the NPT when it opened for signatures in 1968. However, India found itself in a difficult situation due to the NPT's structure.[8] The treaty established a two-tier system: countries that tested a nuclear device before 1 January 1967 were recognised as nuclear weapon states and allowed to retain their nuclear arsenals. This included China, which had tested its first bomb in 1964. Countries that hadn't tested by 1967 were prohibited from developing or acquiring nuclear weapons. This category included India and the 'two-tiered' system proved highly controversial, as it undermined the treaty's claim to comprehensiveness.

India positioned herself as a dissenting voice on the issue of nuclear non-proliferation, particularly after the treaty came into force. From India's viewpoint, the NPT's results fell short of expectations. While three out of the five permanent members of the UN Security Council (P5) signed the treaty, all five continued conducting nuclear tests even afterwards. The US, the Soviet Union, France, China and the UK collectively conducted hundreds of tests after signing the NPT. This ongoing proliferation by established nuclear powers undermined the treaty's core objective of achieving global nuclear disarmament.

India voiced its concerns about the NPT's discriminatory structure at various international forums, including the United Nations General Assembly, the Nuclear Non-Proliferation Treaty Review Conference and the Conference on Disarmament. However, these efforts to advocate for a more equitable treaty framework proved unsuccessful.[9] As a result, India refused to sign the NPT.

BY THE early 1970s, India faced a growing crisis regarding its strategic security. The NPT's inability to prevent the P5 countries—the five permanent members of the UN Security Council (China, France, Russia, the United Kingdom and the US)—from further developing their nuclear arsenals, despite signing the treaty, raised serious concerns for India.

India's security situation was particularly precarious due to its tense relationship with China, a neighbour with whom it had a border conflict in 1962. Notably, China, like India, had not signed the NPT and continued its nuclear weapons programme. These factors likely influenced Indian leaders and scientific experts, leading them to seriously consider developing their own nuclear deterrent.

The 1971 Bangladesh Liberation War was the loudest alarm bell for the decision makers in New Delhi. It highlighted India's security concerns and brought her vulnerabilities into sharp focus.

The deployment of the US aircraft carrier USS Enterprise into the Bay of Bengal during the war, ostensibly to monitor the situation, was widely perceived in India as an attempt to pressure them into a ceasefire unfavourable to their interests.[10]

Several experts believe the 1971 war likely played a significant role in India's decision to revisit the issue of nuclear weapons. This event underscored the limitations of relying solely on conventional military power and the potential strategic benefits of possessing a nuclear deterrent.[11]

AS A result, the Indian leadership shifted gear in 1974 and conducted a peaceful nuclear explosion, codenamed 'Smiling Buddha' at Pokhran in the Rajasthan desert. The test was widely seen as a response to the perceived shortcomings of the NPT and a signal to the P5 countries. In particular, it demonstrated India's scientific capability to develop nuclear weapons if she chose to.

While the 'Smiling Buddha' test provided India with the strategic option of a non-weaponised nuclear deterrent, looking back, India acted with naivety as the country's ultimate goal remained the dismantling of the 'nuclear apartheid' enshrined in the NPT. Indian leaders hoped 'Smiling Buddha' would reignite focus on the achievement of verifiable disarmament by the P5 countries.[12]

Despite referencing their special responsibility under the NPT to pursue nuclear disarmament, the P5 states have been hesitant to relinquish their nuclear arsenals throughout the NPT negotiations. This reluctance stems from their view of nuclear weapons as a critical deterrent against attack and a symbol of their status as major global powers.[13]

During the 1980s and early 1990s, some Indian leaders and decision makers held a strong belief in the P5 countries' ultimate commitment to the NPT. This belief, perhaps misplaced, drove India's continued efforts to bring all parties to the negotiating table.[14]

While China's ongoing nuclear programme was widely acknowledged, India was caught off guard by Pakistan's success in developing both uranium enrichment capability and, subsequently, nuclear weapons.[15] Despite these developments—China's ongoing nuclear programme and Pakistan's acquisition of nuclear capabilities—India, perhaps wrongly, persisted in advocating for the NPT's full implementation.

The penny finally dropped for India in May 1995.

The indefinite extension of the NPT marked a turning point for India's perspective. India criticised the decision, arguing that it perpetuated an unequal system that 'disarmed the unarmed' while allowing nuclear weapon states to maintain their arsenals, rather than pursuing genuine global nuclear disarmament.[16]

India faced another surprise on 10 September 1996, when the General Assembly adopted the Comprehensive Nuclear Test Ban Treaty (CTBT) and opened it for signature.[17]

Another development that compounded India's vulnerability was the collapse of the Soviet Union in 1989. Policymakers and Indian leaders were conscious of the enormous impact on India's security scenario, as India had lost a key security counterweight to the US during the Cold War. This left a weakened Russia and a unipolar world order, which India perceived as potentially detrimental to its own security interests.[18]

IN STARK contrast to China's rapid ascent to nuclear power status, India's path was a protracted, complex and often halting process. Unlike China, which abruptly shifted gears from downplaying nuclear weapons to acquiring them in a short timeframe, India's journey unfolded over several decades, marked by internal debates, shifting priorities and external pressures.[19]

India's flirtation with nuclear testing stretched back to at least 1989, casting a long shadow over the decade. The nation's nuclear programme remained shrouded in secrecy; it was a closely guarded project. Information was tightly controlled, and funding was reportedly hidden within the government's annual budget allocations to the Planning Commission. This budgetary sleight-of-hand masked the true purpose—fuelling the nuclear programme under the broad and unassuming category of 'science and technology.' This opacity fuelled international suspicion and heightened tensions, particularly with neighbouring Pakistan, which was also suspected of pursuing nuclear weapons.[20]

HOWEVER, THE COUNTRY'S political landscape during this period proved to be a significant hurdle. With a revolving door in New Delhi, witnessing seven different prime ministers holding office throughout the 1990s, India's nuclear ambitions faced a period of indecision. This political flux made it difficult to forge a national consensus on the sensitive issue of nuclear testing, ultimately delaying the pivotal decision until May 1998.[21]

The political landscape shifted dramatically in March 1998, with the Bharatiya Janata Party (BJP) led by Prime Minister Atal Bihari Vajpayee coming to power. This change marked a turning point for India's nuclear programme. The new BJP government, with a more nationalistic stance, viewed nuclear weapons as crucial for ensuring national security. Within a remarkably short timeframe—just two months—they organised a series of nuclear tests. Reports suggest that the approval for preparations for these tests likely occurred in April 1998, further highlighting the BJP government's decisive action on this critical issue. India ultimately conducted five nuclear tests in May 1998, sending shockwaves around the world.[22]

THE SWIFT execution of the nuclear tests within just two months of the new government taking office, has been attributed to the tireless efforts of a key figure—the sherpa. This individual, acting as a behind-the-scenes negotiator and strategist, had been a long-time advocate for India's nuclear ambitions. The sherpa's relentless work, likely involving years of planning and preparation, laid the groundwork for the BJP government's decisive action.[23]

The sherpa who implemented the operational part of the pivotal initiative was Avul Pakir Jainulabdeen Abdul Kalam (Dr A P J Abdul Kalam). Born in Rameswaram in 1931, Dr Kalam earned degrees in physics and aerospace engineering before joining DRDO in 1958. His rapid rise saw him become director of a key defence lab by 1979 and scientific advisor to the defence minister in 1983.[24]

Appointed as the chief scientific advisor to the Prime Minister in 1992, Dr Kalam became a pivotal figure in India's scientific and military advancement. He played a central role in overseeing the development of both India's nuclear weapons programme and its potent ballistic missiles. However, his contributions extended beyond the nuclear realm. Dr Kalam also served as the project director for the successful development of SLV-3, India's first satellite launch vehicle. His leadership is widely credited with significantly propelling India's missile programme, ultimately leading the country to achieve Intermediate Range Ballistic Missile (IRBM) capability.[25]

'He was one of the most exuberant boosters of the country's nuclear programme,' wrote *The New York Times*. As the DRDO secretary from 1992 to 1999, he played a key role in the Pokhran-II nuclear tests, solidifying India's position as a nuclear-armed state.[26]

Dr Kalam reportedly advocated India's nuclear weapons programme, believing it to be a deterrent against potential attacks from Pakistan. He also saw the potential for peaceful applications of nuclear technology, such as power generation and advancements in medical treatment.

When the crunch time came, the sherpa was right there and raring to go. Dr Kalam's crucial role in India's nuclear programme solidified his reputation as a leading figure in the field.

While serving as scientific advisor to Defence Minister George Fernandes, Dr Kalam played a key role in convincing Prime Minister Vajpayee to initiate the induction of nuclear weapons into India's arsenal. This episode highlights the importance of advisors with deep technical expertise and the confidence to advocate their beliefs, a quality that sherpas in the Amrit Kaal initiative should strive for.

'It gives us the confidence that we are capable of designing any kind of missile,' Dr Kalam said on the occasion of the first successful Agni launch in 1989. 'We must think and act like a nation of a billion people and not like a million people ... Dream! Dream! Dream!' he had said just after the nuclear tests in 1998.[27]

Dr Kalam not only successfully conducted the tests but surprised Western intelligence agencies, who were not aware of the development until the public announcement on Indian television. This achievement was described by a senior US intelligence official as a 'master stroke of denial and deception.'

In a written statement before the Indian Parliament on 27 May 1998, Prime Minister Vajpayee attributed the responsibility for India's nuclear tests to the countries that already possessed nuclear weapons. He argued that these countries had 'stubbornly refused' to negotiate any treaty requiring the dismantling of their nuclear arsenals.'[28]

INDIA'S 1998 nuclear tests reverberated globally, showcasing the country's arrival as a nuclear power. Yet, the scientific feat was just the first act. The real challenge loomed large: that of gaining the world's trust as a responsible steward of nuclear power. Convincing the international community of India's commitment to disarmament and non-proliferation would be a far steeper climb than mastering nuclear fission.

The Indian Government anticipated 'international condemnation and possible economic sanctions in the wake of the nuclear tests. However, they believed these repercussions were necessary to achieve the strategic goals of the initiative and safeguard India's security.

The international community's response to India's nuclear tests in 1998 was swift and critical, escalating into a new crisis.

The US, citing the Glenn Amendment, immediately imposed economic sanctions on India. These sanctions restricted both access to technology and economic trade.

Japan strongly condemned India's actions and implemented similar economic sanctions.

Australia also took measures, but unlike the US and Japan, they did not impose trade or investment sanctions. New Zealand expressed its disapproval by recalling its High Commissioner from India.[29]

RECOGNISING THE gravity of the international response, the Indian Government adopted a proactive approach to engage with the international community and governments. This new crisis demanded a fresh diplomatic strategy, requiring a new sherpa with different skill sets to navigate the challenges and find solutions swiftly.

Despite having several capable ministers, including a strong Defence Minister, and holding the Foreign Affairs portfolio himself, Prime Minister Vajpayee sought a trusted and skilled diplomat for this critical task. He identified Jaswant Singh, the deputy chairman of the Planning Commission, as a suitable candidate.

This is a crucial learning for the success of new pivotal initiatives during Amrit Kaal—the selection of a capable and trusted sherpa is paramount.

Following the controversial nuclear tests in 1998, India faced international pressure to formally articulate its nuclear doctrine. In response, the government released its official Nuclear Doctrine in January 2003. This doctrine outlined India's approach to nuclear weapons and aimed to reassure the international community.[30]

Singh, known for his articulation and diplomatic acumen, was entrusted to explain India's position to the international community. His primary objective was to convince world leaders about the rationale behind the tests and stress on India's commitment to peaceful nuclear deterrence and the 'No First Use' policy. He needed to effectively communicate India's perspective on sovereignty, security concerns and the principle of equity in the global nuclear order.[31]

AS A special envoy, Jaswant Singh embarked on a diplomatic offensive, travelling to the US and other key countries to engage in discussions with leaders.[32]

Jaswant Singh's decision to engage with Strobe Talbott, the US Deputy Secretary of State, proved to be a strategic move. Talbott later recounted Jaswant Singh's singular focus on finding common ground, a point underscored by their 14 meetings across seven countries.[33] These discussions, known as the Singh–Talbott dialogue, addressed core issues. Singh sought the removal of sanctions and international recognition of India's nuclear status. Talbott, however, pressed for India to commit to five key benchmarks, including defining its nuclear doctrine, size of arsenal and confidence-building measures with Pakistan.

While Talbott initially believed the US held the upper hand, Singh's perseverance appeared to have worn down American resolve. Over time, international interest in sanctions waned. Additionally, the US Congress cast doubt on the Comprehensive Test Ban Treaty, a factor that had originally prompted India's tests. Ultimately, President Clinton himself emphasised the need for a new approach. Despite initial scepticism towards Singh, Clinton became determined to visit India and forge a path toward cooperation.[34]

Jaswant Singh's hope was that by the dialogue's conclusion, or ideally, through its permanent resolution, the US and India would find common ground on fundamental issues. He also aimed to develop a framework for managing disagreements effectively, thereby, embarking on a mission to mend the fractured US–India relationship.

In the aftermath of the nuclear tests, the Indian Government demonstrated adept crisis management. It swiftly engaged with allies and partners, diligently explaining its rationale behind the tests. Additionally, it pursued measures to de-escalate tensions with Pakistan, culminating in a civil nuclear agreement with the US. These successful diplomatic efforts stand as a testament to Indian statesmanship and serve as a valuable model for navigating future international crises.

THOUGH THE initial sherpa's efforts culminated in the successful nuclear tests, his successor secured a distinct diplomatic victory for India. This victory paved the way for India's gradual integration into the global nuclear order.[35]

Jaswant Singh's diplomacy proved instrumental in achieving the government's initial goal of reassuring the world of India's responsible nuclear stance. This success stemmed, in part, from the mutual respect between Singh and Talbott, the US deputy secretary of state. Their respectful dialogue paved the way for a significant transformation in India–US relations.[36]

Defying global expectations, India's 1998 nuclear tests ultimately paved the way for a landmark agreement with the US—the Indo-US nuclear deal. This historic deal brought India significant benefits and advantages previously reserved for established nuclear powers.[37]

THE 2005 US-India Civil Nuclear Agreement, often simply called the 'nuclear deal,' was perhaps the culmination of tireless efforts by two key sherpas who persevered with unwavering support from their respective political leaders, even as governments changed due to India's democratic elections.

On 1 October 2008, the US Congress finally gave its stamp of approval to the US–India Civil Nuclear Agreement, a landmark deal that ushered in a new era of cooperation between the two nations.[38] The Indo-US nuclear deal had been years in the making, requiring painstaking negotiations between US and Indian officials. It marked a significant shift in US foreign policy, as it allowed for civil nuclear cooperation with a country that wasn't a signatory to the NPT.[39]

The 'nuclear deal' proved a game changer, as it opened the closed door of the club of the multilateral export control group, which regulates the global trade in high technologies and strategic goods.

With comprehensive implementation of the pivotal initiative of India's security, successive Indian governments continued with the consolidation process. India became a member of various entities that further provided a chance to play the big game.

In a significant step towards bolstering its missile technology credentials and integration into global non-proliferation regimes, India secured membership in the Missile Technology Control

Regime (MTCR) in 2016. This achievement was the culmination of years of persistent diplomatic efforts. The MTCR membership allows India to participate in legitimate missile technology transfers and fosters international cooperation in controlling the proliferation of certain types of missiles.[40]

India's subsequent acquisition of membership in other export control regimes, such as the Australia Group (AG) in January 2018 and the Wassenaar Arrangement (WA) in December 2017 reflects its commitment to responsible international trade in sensitive technologies.[41]

Similarly, at the strategic front, New Delhi has made impressive advances toward deploying a nuclear triad of land-, air-, and sea-based assets in keeping with the objectives of its doctrine, which is to build a Credible Minimum Deterrence (CMD) and maintain an 'Assured Second Strike Capability'.[42]

With the testing of the new Agni-P medium-range ballistic missile on 18 December 2021, India has achieved what is called 'backward integration' of technology by not only increasing the range of ballistic missiles but also replacing older technologies with more advanced technologies.[43]

India's strategic nuclear cooperation agreements with countries such as the US, France, Russia and Australia have been instrumental in bolstering its civilian nuclear programme. These agreements provide India with access to vital civilian nuclear technology and fuel essential to meet its expanding energy demands. Additionally, they have fostered closer ties with partner nations.

THE 1998 nuclear tests under the Vajpayee government weren't just a scientific feat; they were also a calculated gamble for global influence. This audacious move fundamentally altered India's strategic posture, projecting an image of strength and deterrence. The resulting sense of security arguably propelled India towards a coveted seat at the 'high table' of international politics.

Prime Minister Vajpayee's visionary leadership during this period is underscored in his interview to *India Today*: 'We do not want to cover our action with a veil of needless ambiguity,' Mr Vajpayee had said. 'India is now a nuclear weapons state. We have the capacity for a big bomb now, for which a necessary command-and-control system is also in place. Ours will never be weapons of aggression.'[44]

***

India's 'New Deal'

Infrastructure Development through Public–Private Partnership

Meanwhile, New Delhi has made progress in urban governance. Although the haze is still serious, the distinctive smells that hit you as soon as you stepped off the plane four years ago has generally disappeared.

—**Zhang Jiadong**
Director, CSAS, Fudan University, China
(*Global Times*, 2 January 2024)[1]

Today is a historic day for Mumbai and Maharashtra, along with the resolve for 'Viksit Bharat.' Today, the nation has received Atal Setu, one of the longest sea bridges in the world.

— **Prime Minister Narendra Modi**
12 January 2024

I LEFT India for Sydney in Australia in 1994 from New Delhi's Indira Gandhi International Airport, three years after the economic reforms of 1991.

The drive to the airport was an assault on my senses. Headlights in the smog-choked lanes to the airport, illuminated dust motes dancing in the oily air. Loud horns and shouts competed for dominance in the cacophony. At the terminal, the chaos had reached a fever pitch. Impatient people pressed against each other, bathed in sweat. Luggage trolleys clattered like runaway shopping carts. It could have been a scene straight out of a Lagos market, not the gateway to an international flight as I'd envisioned.

After settling in Australia, I joined an international energy company as a senior executive, and flew to Jakarta in 1995 for various meetings—only six months after leaving India.

Stepping off the plane at Jakarta International Airport, I was struck by its gleaming cleanliness and the courteous professionalism of the staff at the airport. The smooth ride on a six-lane highway to my hotel underscored the impressive development underway in Indonesia.

It made me realise that I didn't need to read *The Wall Street Journal* or *The Economist* to know how far some of the Asian Tigers had progressed. It was clear why India was still perceived as a land of snake charmers, and why most Asian Tigers, including Indonesia, were clearly on their way to becoming modern, prosperous countries.

I naturally expected Sydney's infrastructure to be vastly

superior to cities in India, as Australia is a developed economy. However, my trip to Jakarta made me think about the factors that influence how different countries attract foreign investment and why India was struggling immediately after opening up the economy in 1991.

Was the complete lack of reliable world class infrastructure a crucial factor?

In Jakarta, I saw a city that was clean, orderly and well-maintained. The roads were wide and well-paved, transportation was efficient and the people were friendly and helpful. In contrast, in India the roads were congested and potholed, public transportation was overcrowded and unreliable, and commuters were often rude and unhelpful due to the scarcity of seats on buses and trains.

INDIA, AT the time of the economic reforms, had all the hallmarks of poor, crippling infrastructure across the spectrum—from roads, airports and shipping ports to unreliable electricity supply.[2] Those of us who lived in Delhi in the 1980s, as I did while studying at IIT Delhi, can attest to the jaw-dropping reality of India's poor infrastructure.

The main reason for it was the approach India took for building its infrastructure. Since Independence, Indian policymakers and government treated infrastructure as a routine exercise, and largely financed it by allocating a small budget in every five-year plan.[3] As a result, when the economy was opened up, India's poor infrastructure quickly became a major obstacle to attracting investment.

Infrastructure constraints were usually cited by local and foreign investors as a key speed breaker in India's quest to sustain

8 to 9 per cent growth.[4] Foreign businesses wanted assurance that they would be able to operate their businesses efficiently, and India's poor infrastructure was raising several red flags for them.

This led to inadequate addition of new capacity as well as poor quality of service in all major infrastructure sectors, including railways, roads, ports, and electricity generation and distribution. In addition, corruption and lack of transparency contributed to a poor state of Indian infrastructure in general. It also discouraged private investors from participating in infrastructure projects.[5]

The crisis of poor existing infrastructure became even more dire with the substantial increase in population in the 1980s and 1990s. Migration of poor people in large numbers from villages to cities in search of livelihood added extra pressure to the existing poor infrastructure, particularly to roads, trains and electricity.[6]

The crisis in the power sector of infrastructure was equally dire in India. The power sector has had severe functional problems resulting in State Electricity Boards (SEBs) struggling under resource crunches and operating at huge commercial losses.[7]

The cascading failures of India's electricity grid in the 1990s and the early part of the twenty-first century, such as the 2001 Western Regional Grid collapse, serve as grim reminders of how infrastructure failures could disrupt entire economies and cost lives. It has a devastating impact on businesses across the board.[8]

Unreliable electricity supply particularly impacted the operations of most small- and medium-scale businesses or enterprises (SMEs) and firms, because these businesses normally don't have budget for alternative sources such as diesel power generators. Uncertainty due to irregular supply of electricity negatively affects the total factor productivity and labour productivity of manufacturing SMEs.[9]

India's 1991 economic liberalisation reforms promised

opportunities for growth, but many SMEs were left behind. Lacking access to necessary resources and facing significant challenges such as frequent power outages, these SMEs remained stunted in their development. Power outages, in particular, had a crippling effect on productivity. Unable to operate machinery or complete tasks, workers sat idle, while businesses incurred additional costs and ultimately passed them on to customers in the form of higher prices. This not only eroded profits, but also hampered employment generation, as SMEs traditionally rely heavily on a semi-skilled workforce.[10]

SMEs incurred higher costs due to power outages, as they had to purchase backup generators or pay for expensive overtime work. It had a direct impact on their bottom line, making it difficult for them to compete with larger businesses and overseas imports, including from China. As a result, the imports from China skyrocketed.[11]

Therefore, it is no surprise that India struggled to attract international investment for a long time, while the Asian Tigers—China and Korea—galloped ahead. It is now widely accepted that infrastructure investments have been one of the main drivers of China's rapid economic growth.[12] The impact of poor infrastructure on India's GDP growth has been significant and it has been estimated to be pulled down by 1 to 2 per cent every year.[13]

A WELL-maintained and efficient transportation network, coupled with a reliable energy grid and a robust telecommunications system, not only demonstrates a government's commitment to long-term development, but also directly incentivises investors by facilitating low-cost production through reduced transportation expenses, increased energy efficiency and improved communication channels. This, in turn, enhances a country's market competitiveness and attracts further investment.[14]

Several Asian countries commenced building new and efficient infrastructure through a variety of financing options as early as the mid-1980s.[15]

To bridge India's infrastructure deficit at the time of the 1991 balance of payments crisis, the International Monetary Fund (IMF) and other international agencies encouraged India to make serious efforts to attract and mobilise private investment in infrastructure. To address this problem, India needed to adopt a policy-driven approach to attract private investment in infrastructure.

India, finally, took her first step in October 1994 when the Department of Economic Affairs, under the Minister of Finance, set up an Expert Group for an analysis of all aspects of commercialisation of infrastructure projects. This group was to work extensively and published a comprehensive report that strongly advocated a significant role for private capital in India's infrastructure development, particularly for promotion of public–private partnerships (PPP) and pathways for commercialisation of infrastructure.

The goal of this exercise was to identify the specific skills needed for attracting private investment and drive successful PPP projects in infrastructure. However, the results yielded nothing more than generic platitudes and thus failed to address the crucial challenges of a skill shortage within the bureaucracy for designing and implementing a successful PPP project.[16]

Consequently, potential investors remained uninspired.

FIVE YEARS after the report was published, the Indian Government made its first serious attempt in 2001 to improve the country's infrastructure by conceptualising and executing a network of highways connecting India's four main metropolitan cities, namely Delhi, Mumbai, Chennai and Kolkata, under a PPP model. This project, known as the Golden Quadrilateral (GQ), was the largest highway project ever undertaken by India, and was aimed at improving North-South and East-West (NS-EW) corridors with port connectivity, and other projects in phases.[17]

Interestingly, the GQ project was completed successfully and under budget, costing only half of the project cost estimated at the time of planning.[18] Public servants and policymakers involved in the landmark infrastructure project touted its completion far under budget.

It finally became clear that the joint secretaries in both the infrastructure ministry and the finance ministry had overlooked a more serious problem: a profound shortage of skills in every aspect of infrastructure creation, including project design, cost estimation, land acquisition constraints, and policies for effective implementation.

Many in the government underestimated the intricacies of attracting private players to infrastructure projects, including understanding that securing participation of private players hinges on a delicate balance—offering attractive returns, while carefully mitigating inherent risks.[19]

THE GOVERNMENT'S long-standing dominance in public infrastructure, coupled with entrenched bureaucracy and resistance to change from incumbent officials, significantly hampered efforts to build the necessary skills for new industries.[20]

Nevertheless, India witnessed disproportionate manufacturing growth along the corridor along the GQ. This highlighted firsthand the critical role of infrastructure in economic expansion. This provided successive governments the incentive to prioritise ambitious projects for unlocking a new era of prosperity. The Eleventh Plan (2008–2012) saw a commitment to massive infrastructure investments—nearly US $500 billion.[21]

INDIA DESPERATELY needed a game-changing pivotal initiative to turbocharge physical infrastructure development. It craved a determined leader, a sherpa with unwavering grit, to shepherd this critical undertaking to fruition. The persistent underperformance of projects forced decision makers to confront the significant challenges of implementation.

As India grappled with infrastructure bottlenecks that threatened to stifle its economic growth, a beacon of hope emerged in the form of a visionary civil servant. Working tirelessly within the system ever since his initial involvement in 1993, Gajendra Haldea meticulously navigated the complexities of the PPP model, transforming it from a near-theoretical concept in the Indian context into a powerful engine for progress. He thus became the sherpa who ended up becoming the 'good and fair tsar' of infrastructure in India. He has well and truly been called the 'Father of India's Infrastructure.'[22]

After graduating in Economics and Law at the University of Rajasthan, he embarked on a distinguished career in the Indian Administrative Service, starting in 1973. His first foray into the world of infrastructure began in 1993, when he joined the Finance Ministry as Joint Secretary (infrastructure). Back then, the Indian government was intensifying efforts to attract private investment in infrastructure projects, and the Finance Ministry was mandated with the crucial role.[23]

Before diving into infrastructure, Mr Haldea had already established his brilliance, born from a profound understanding of any issue he tackled.

The Indian government recognised electricity access as a fundamental pillar for rapid economic growth, poverty alleviation, driving industrial development, job creation and improved quality of life for all citizens. Therefore, it opted for allowing private participation, though only in electricity generation, as early as 1992.[24]

However, the government perhaps overlooked two crucial factors—it did not recognise the extent of the skill shortage within the ministry, which hindered its ability to fully understand the ramifications of the new policy. And it failed to factor in the legacy of the existing bureaucracy that had a tendency to hinder the implementation process.

The consequences of these factors came home to roost immediately.

In June 1992, Enron engaged in negotiations with the Indian Government and identified the state of Maharashtra for their first project—the Dabhol Power Project—due to the size of the economy and the population. It was immediately hailed as a beacon of progress in electricity reforms by the government.

Negotiations began in earnest with both the State Government and the Maharashtra State Electricity Board. However, the project soon became embroiled in several controversies, casting a long shadow over reform efforts. Maharashtra state bureaucrats lacked the expertise to assess the financial feasibility of these large-scale projects, leaving them unprepared for the risks associated with foreign currency fluctuations.[25]

The Indian side lacked skills to counter the ever-increasing demands and aggressive tactics of Enron. A battery of Enron lawyers started to propose new conditions in every meeting to safeguard their investment.

Following lengthy negotiations, the Maharashtra Government agreed to a 32 per cent return for Enron due to an alleged double counting of foreign exchange risk.[26]

The Enron management remained uneasy about the project and put forward a new condition for a counter-guarantee by the Indian Government.

At this stage, the Finance Ministry, where Mr Haldea was then working, got involved with the Dabhol Power Project. The Maharashtra political system was pressurising the Finance Ministry to approve the Enron project by giving a counter-guarantee for any shortfall in power purchase from the power plant. They requested a full government guarantee for the project.

Mr Haldea recognised the risks of a counter-guarantee, not due to deep experience in PPP—he was as new to the 'new game' as anyone else—but due to his dedication to the nation's wellbeing. He devised innovative financing structures (or counter-guarantees) that protected the Central Government's finances while enabling Maharashtra to move forward with the projects.

His foresight proved valuable when the power project failed, saving the Indian Government billions. Notably, his meticulous work on the counter-guarantee protected the public interest in ways the Power Ministry had seemingly overlooked.[27]

MR HALDEA immediately recognised that the intricate legal, financial and technical aspects of PPP projects demanded a level of expertise that government officials often lack, potentially leading to unintended consequences.

He zoomed his focus on electricity reforms and worked

tirelessly on what eventually resulted in the Electricity Act of 2003. This act was hailed as a signature achievement for the Indian power sector, ushering in a new era of market-driven competition. This shift away from negotiated agreements with investors aimed to improve efficiency and attract private investment in generation and transmission, ultimately aiming to address the country's growing energy needs.

HIS EXCELLENT work and dedication as a sherpa didn't go unnoticed. Mr Montek Singh Ahluwalia, Deputy Chairman of the main planning body in India, the Planning Commission, invited him to set up an infrastructure division within the commission. He became head of the Secretariat for Infrastructure and PPP in 2004.[28]

Before joining the Planning Commission, Mr Haldea had worked on and subsequently published the first Model Concession Agreement (MCA) for national highways in 2000. This MCA became a template for all future MCAs in various other areas of infrastructure.[29]

He realised early on that every member of the secretariat was learning on the job. So, he adopted open-mindedness and earnestly engaged with his team. He actively challenged assumptions and fostered constructive dialogue by never dismissing ideas outright. Instead, he posed insightful questions, demonstrating a genuine interest in understanding diverse perspectives. This approach not only promoted collaboration, but also led to breakthrough solutions. For instance, his keen questioning during a complex operation briefing uncovered a critical oversight, prompting a strategic shift that ultimately saved the mission.

What elevated his accomplishments was his dedication to

building expertise from the ground up. Having first mastered the intricacies of the PPP model, he then adapted it to fit the specific needs of India. His collaborative working style stood out. Instead of dismissing suggestions outright, he would probe gently with clarifying questions, indicating a genuine interest in understanding the suggestion. This interactive approach not only helped him grasp issues, but also empowered others to articulate their ideas and potentially spark breakthroughs themselves.

This meticulous approach and unwavering commitment could prove invaluable for India during the Amrit Kaal initiative.

Laying the groundwork for private sector involvement in infrastructure, his team spearheaded the creation of a comprehensive PPP framework. This began with standardised bidding documents and technical specifications for PPP projects. Streamlining the appraisal and approval processes further bolstered efficiency. The resulting framework prioritised transparency, accountability and efficiency in project execution. To facilitate this, the team developed model concession agreements encompassing diverse infrastructure sectors such as power, highways, ports, airports, railways and land use, with specific examples like the Hyderabad Metro Rail.[30]

The National Highway Development Programme was a flagship programme to upgrade and expand India's national highway network. The programme utilised the PPP model extensively, attracting private investment for the development and maintenance of highways.

Haldea 'batted from both ends of a cricket pitch.' From one end, he was taking care of governmental responsibility and from the other end, he was playing for private investors.

Haldea's work in project monitoring and implementation was instrumental in the success of many PPP projects in India.

He was able to identify and address potential problems early on, which helped to keep projects on track and on budget. He also worked closely with project stakeholders to ensure that everyone was on the same page and that there was a clear understanding of project goals.

To increase the viability of the 'greenfield' project, Haldea was instrumental in designing and implementing the Viability Gap Funding scheme, which provides financial support from the government to attract private sector investment. This scheme bridges the gap between the cost of a project and the revenue it is expected to generate, making it more attractive to private investors.

In the years since, the number of PPP projects in India has grown significantly. In 2018, the government awarded 1,000 PPP projects worth Rs 3.5 lakh crores. This represents a significant increase from the early days of PPPs in India, when the government awarded only a handful of projects each year.

The future of PPPs for infrastructure in India is bright. The government is committed to promoting PPPs and the number of PPP projects is expected to grow in the coming years. PPPs have the potential to play a major role in infrastructure development in India and they can help to bridge the funding gap, bring in expertise and experience of the private sector and accelerate the delivery of infrastructure projects.

The current government has identified PPPs as a key strategy for infrastructure development. The National Infrastructure Pipeline envisages an investment of Rs 111 lakh crores from 2020 to 2025 and PPPs are expected to play a major role in delivering this investment.

THE PIVOTAL initiative for the National Infrastructure PPP programme was successfully implemented with the core framework in place, and with key government officials equipped with the necessary expertise. Establishing comprehensive policies and regulations emerged as the next logical step to ensure its continued success.

After a tentative start in 1992, successive Indian governments have ensured that PPP projects are successful and on track to deliver the benefits that they are intended to.

And that's an important lesson for designing an initiative to tackle a crisis during Amrit Kaal.

The PPP model has been used to deliver a wide range of infrastructure projects, including roads, railways, airports, ports, power plants and water treatment plants in India.

The UPA government in 2005 launched a policy framework for the development and regulation of the power sector in India, called the National Power Policy (NPP), using the PPP model. The NPP has had a significant impact on the power sector in India. The reforms have led to increased private sector investment in the sector, improved efficiency and reduced costs. The NPP has also helped to reduce the power deficit in India.

In 2022, the current Modi government established a new organisation under the Department of Economic Affairs, Ministry of Finance, Government of India. This is the Infrastructure Finance Secretariat (IFS). Its main objective is facilitating and enhancing the infrastructure financing ecosystem in India and is designed to play a key role in catalysing infrastructure investment in India. It will do this by providing a single window for infrastructure finance, promoting PPPs and building capacity in the infrastructure finance sector. In addition, it has developed a National Infrastructure Finance Roadmap, which outlines the government's strategy for infrastructure finance.

The Viability Gap Funding scheme (VGF) has been

successful in attracting private investment in a number of major infrastructure projects, including roads, railways, airports and power plants and has helped to improve the country's infrastructure and boost economic growth.

The VGF was set up by the current government in 2020 and is a financial mechanism used by governments to bridge the gap between the cost of an infrastructure project and the revenue that the project is expected to generate. VGF can be provided in a variety of forms such as grants, loans and equity investments.

The objective of VGF is to make infrastructure projects more financially attractive to private investors. By providing VGF, governments can reduce the risks associated with infrastructure projects and encourage private investors to participate in these projects.

The National Monetisation Pipeline (NMP) is a plan by the current Indian Government to monetise its assets over a four-year period from FY2022 to FY2025. The NMP aims to raise Rs 6 lakh crores (US$80 billion) through the monetisation of assets across sectors such as roads, railways, power, airports and telecom.

THE RECENT inauguration of the 21.8 km-long Atal Setu bridge on 13 January 2024 signifies a significant milestone in implementing the PPP model for infrastructure in India. This achievement undoubtedly reflects the foresight and efforts of individuals such as Gajendra Haldea, the true sherpa for this key pivotal initiative.[31]

***

Digital Identity to Billions
Aadhaar

My only identity is Infosys. I will be going to lead a programme to give identity to every Indian. But today I am losing my identity.

—**Nandan Nilekani**
Infosys Chairman, 2009[1]

INTRODUCED DURING World War II, the humble ration card had evolved into a vital tool for identifying over 1 billion citizens in India for 70 years![2]

But how did this food distribution device morph into a crucial identification (ID) document?

The ration card's journey reflects the complex interplay of historical events, government policies and citizens' needs.

In the immediate aftermath of the Partition, ration cards emerged as a lifeline, helping manage the large-scale displacement of people and food shortages. However, their usefulness extended far beyond those initial years. As government policies and economic practices evolved, a critical gap emerged—a lack of comprehensive and verifiable documentation for the entire Indian population. The ration card, once a temporary measure, stepped in to fill this void, becoming an essential document for countless citizens. While not without limitations, it became an essential indicator of residential status and, by extension, identity. Its accessibility made it valuable for various purposes, including proving residential status for housing benefits and government subsidies. The multifaceted evolution and long-term use of ration cards fostered public trust and thereby their acceptance as legitimate identification documents.[3]

THERE WERE, nevertheless, unintended consequences of evolution of the ration card as a proxy to a pan-India ID card. It has indeed given birth to several crises throughout India's journey of 75 years as a nation-state.

India's booming population exposed a critical weakness in the ration card system—the lack of a robust identity verification mechanism. This meant social programmes intended for the most vulnerable often missed reaching them. Without proper record-keeping and verification, two key problems emerged. Some individuals managed to exploit the system, receiving benefits multiple times. This diverted resources away from those who truly needed them. Ineligible individuals, due to weak verification, received benefits meant for the most disadvantaged. This created inefficiency and frustration within the system.[4]

The crisis was recognised as early as 1985 when Rajiv Gandhi, India's sixth prime minister, reported to have said in a public rally that only 15 paise of every rupee spent by the government on welfare and poverty alleviation reached the intended beneficiary.[5] He, perhaps, was stating the main reason why successive governments could not make a dent in India's poverty.

Government subsidies encompassing basic requirements of everyday living have been the backbone of India's political economy since Independence. The quantum of subsidies grew from Rs 1.22 billion in 1991 to Rs 1.73 trillion in 2010. According to the World Bank, government subsidies in India amounted to $US100 billion in 2019. This is equivalent to about 2 per cent of India's GDP. The largest subsidies relate to food, fertiliser and petroleum products.[6]

Another aspect of the crisis was that poor and deserving citizens could not avail of social programmes because they could not pay the required bribes to the government officials for their inclusion in government records.

Beyond inefficient delivery, over time, the endemic corruption entrenched itself within the system, affecting India's growth. Social scientists and economists concur that since Independence, rampant corruption has been a significant factor hindering poverty reduction, and thereby the country's growth, because it diverts resources meant for essential services such as education, healthcare and infrastructure, thereby leading to poverty and widening inequality.[7]

Inadequate targeting, rampant corruption and leakages of funds crippled India's subsidy system, preventing the poor from claiming what was rightfully theirs. Official estimates indicate that in 2011–12, 41 per cent of the kerosene subsidy, 15 per cent of the rice subsidy, 54 per cent of the wheat subsidy and 48 per cent of the sugar subsidy were lost as leakage. This represented a staggering loss of public funds, and indicated the system required an immediate fix.[8]

ANOTHER DIMENSION of the crisis that was growing rapidly was unregulated migration across the subcontinent's borders. A case study of undocumented migration from Bangladesh to India indicates the severity of the situation.[9] According to Census 2001 data, there were 314 million migrants, and out of these, migrants from Bangladesh were around 10–20 million, which is the largest share of migrants from any other country to India.

Influx of a large number of migrants, coupled with endemic corruption, hampered access to government services for legitimate residents. Initially, the border states bore the brunt of the illegal migration, but the impact soon rippled into megacities such as Mumbai and Delhi.

SUCCESSIVE GOVERNMENTS were aware of an urgent need for a robust system for identifying citizens for benefits and other social programmes and making commitments to deliver subsidies to genuine citizens. But every government opted for 'kicking the issue into the long grass.'

The loudest wake-up call for a nationwide verifiable ID card for the citizen came from the Kargil War, which originated from an attack by Pakistan in the Kargil area of Jammu & Kashmir state in 1999. The local administration and the Indian government in Delhi were both caught napping and failed to detect large-scale intrusion from Pakistan into the Kargil area.[10]

In the aftermath of the Kargil War, the then Prime Minister Atal Bihari Vajpayee established a committee to study the shortcomings in defence preparedness exposed by the conflict and glean valuable lessons. This committee aimed to formulate concrete measures to bolster India's preparedness and effectively counter similar future occurrences. The committee emphasised the need for secure and verifiable ID cards for Indian citizens in border areas, citing national security concerns. This recommendation aimed to emulate the nationwide identity card system being implemented at the time.

A separate group of ministers, tasked with studying the committee's recommendations, submitted a report in 2001 titled 'Reforming the National Security System.'[11]

The Vajpayee government lost power in the 2004 election.

Echoing Victor Hugo's sentiment that 'nothing is more powerful than an idea whose time has come,' the drive to establish a unique identity system for all Indian citizens transcended political change in Delhi.

The new government started the next step of the pivotal initiative in earnest. Despite a change in government in 2004, the initiative persisted, demonstrating its perceived importance and potential impact.

The initiative's fascinating evolution offers valuable lessons for Amrit Kaal. It demonstrates the inherent limitations of the idea of pre-planning every aspect of such a complex endeavour. As circumstances evolve, the initiative's scope can be strategically adjusted and potentially integrated with other relevant issues, enhancing its overall impact.

INDIA'S POLICY implementation landscape presents myriad complexities. The national identity card project, for instance, encountered initial delays, with the nodal agency being established three years after several setbacks in February 2009.

The initial focus of efforts was on poor families living below the poverty line (BPL). In March 2006, a project entitled 'Unique Identification for BPL Families' was approved to provide unique identification numbers to families living below the poverty line.

Soon after, a committee was formed to design how data would be managed in the system. This committee's work led to a broader vision for a national identification system, resulting in the creation of a ministerial group in December 2006. This group aimed to combine the existing projects and create a single identification system for all Indian residents.[12]

AS THE broader contours of a 'national identity project' were slowly taking shape in the corridors of Indian policymaking in Delhi, down south in the 'information technology capital of India'—Bangalore—someone was already thinking about how to deliver the technology for good governance to the Indian system. Nandan Nilekani, who was running the most successful IT outsourcing company, Infosys, since 2002, decided to hand over the reins to the younger generation to focus on writing a book. The book was aimed to lay out in detail his confidence in the potential of information technology for reforming Indian shortcomings in education, inequality and urban infrastructure.

After leaving Infosys, Nandan Nilekani channelled his vision for India's future into a book titled *Imagining India,* published in late 2008. A key theme of the book was Nilekani's advocacy for a unique ID system for all Indian citizens, which he believed would be crucial for the country's development.

It sparked reactions beyond mere CEO ruminations, according to Pratap Bhanu Mehta, head of the Delhi thinktank Centre for Policy Research. Mehta hailed the book as emblematic of a burgeoning Indian optimism: 'Only in the recent decade has a generation in India truly embraced the belief that the future holds far greater promise than the past.'

Nilekani had a successful promotional tour of his book in the US and returned to India with the intention of continuing his co-chairman role at Infosys. However, destiny had something new planned for him.[13]

The 2009 election provided the mandate to the United Progressive Alliance and presented an excellent opportunity to bring the national identity project into sharp focus from the backburner.

THE NEW government led by Dr Manmohan Singh gauged the complexity of the pivotal initiative and had the foresight to find a sherpa. He wanted a qualified leader to manage the implementation process. While the extent of Dr Singh's familiarity with Nilekani's book remains unclear, evidence suggests he actively sought a suitable individual to lead the project. He was successful in securing Nandan Nilekani's agreement to lead the initiative and appointed him the first Chairman of the Unique Identification Authority of India (UIDAI).[14]

Nilekani demonstrated his farsightedness and deep understanding of politics and the working style of the power corridors in New Delhi when he insisted on a five-year term and a cabinet-level post as UIDAI chairman. His intention was to create a 'buffer zone' from the inevitable turf wars within the administration.

NILEKANI RELOCATED to Delhi in 2009, which was a new experience for him—from being an IT tsar to being a 'politician' living in a posh villa with 24/7 security at the gate.

A potentially crucial lesson for Amrit Kaal initiatives involves identifying leaders with appropriate skill sets. The Aadhaar project's success in navigating its complex and ambitious nature, particularly its heavy reliance on information technology for security and distributed computing, highlights this importance. The project demanded expertise in biometrics, data security and distributed computing, and its eventual success underscores the value of finding individuals with such specific knowledge and experience.

Nilekani's decision to lead the Aadhaar project was a major turning point in the history of the pivotal initiative. He brought with him a wealth of experience and expertise and was able to build a strong team of professionals to help him deliver the project.

One crucial decision he made was to build UIDAI's technology centre on Bangalore's southern Ring Road. As a true leader, he also created a culture of innovation and collaboration at the UIDAI and Srikanth Nadhamuni as head of technology at UIDAI.[15]

Srikanth had worked in Silicon Valley for 15 years and in

2002, he returned to India and launched a non-profit group that helped strengthen the public databases of city governments with Nilekani. In other words, he had the passion for making a difference in India and he had a 'long tooth' in the tech world.

A strong advocate for the project through his book, Nilekani was expected to excel in navigating the technological aspects of the initiative. However, he exceeded expectations by fostering collaboration and buy-in from diverse stakeholders. He successfully engaged both the government and public servants, securing their support, while also working with the private sector to achieve cost-effective implementation.

However, like most government initiatives, the project encountered significant hurdles from various stakeholders.

When Nandan Nilekani decided to lead his pet project, he might have felt like a pastor interacting with his congregation, particularly because he was handpicked by the Prime Minister of India, himself. This gained him a lot of political capital.

But reality of the 'power corridor' in Delhi hit him hard right from the initial stages when he faced strong opposition to the Aadhaar initiative from various political parties.[16]

One major concern raised by the Bharatiya Janata Party (BJP) centred on the inclusion of all residents in the Aadhaar system. They argued that this could potentially allow individuals who lack Indian citizenship to access government benefits and services.

Left-wing political parties expressed concerns about the Aadhaar initiative, suggesting that it could potentially lead to the exclusion of certain segments of society from accessing government subsidies. They argued that the system might create discriminatory practices against the poor and the underprivileged.

Beyond political opposition, Nilekani encountered concerns from civil society and privacy advocates. These groups expressed apprehensions about the Aadhaar system's potential for extensive data collection on individuals. They argued that this data could be misused for malicious purposes such as harassment or improper surveillance.

Challenges also arose from within the Indian bureaucracy, known for its established procedures and propensity for opaqueness.

The Aadhaar initiative, with its emphasis on transparency and data accessibility, potentially required adjustments to these existing systems. This could have contributed to concerns within the bureaucracy about adapting to new processes and the potential implications for information sharing.

Nilekani was aware of the general challenges involved in such a large undertaking. These challenges, such as technology limitations, public adoption hurdles, or even resistance from different government departments, came from various stakeholders. However, what might have surprised him the most was the unexpected opposition from sections within the Indian National Congress (INC), the party in power at that time. While Nandan and his team were diligently working on building the different aspects of the project, the government apparently began to have doubts and disagreements about the initiative, particularly its expanding scope. This internal party conflict must have come as a shock to Nilekani and his team.

The Congress had originally conceived the Aadhaar initiative and Nandan Nilekani was a member of the party. So, it was certainly a surprise when the Congress started to oppose the initiative.

It is still unknown why Congress decided to go cold on this important initiative. One possibility is that they may have been concerned about the potential political fallout from the Aadhaar initiative. The BJP had been strongly opposing the initiative and the Congress may have been worried that if they continued to support the initiative, they would lose votes to the BJP.

The Congress party struggled to develop a cohesive strategy on Aadhaar due to internal disagreements. Some members voiced concerns about potential privacy breaches inherent in the system. Others saw the potential for Aadhaar to streamline welfare programmes and reduce fraud. This ideological divide made it difficult for Congress to present a unified stance on the issue.

Additionally, Home Minister P Chidambaram reportedly viewed Aadhaar as a potential competitor to his own project, the National Population Register. This internal political dynamic may have further complicated Congress' approach to Aadhaar.[17]

Nandan Nilekani demonstrated supreme clarity of thought and the commitment expected of an executor of a pivotal initiative. Although he was relatively new to political manoeuvring, he devised an astute plan for outwitting the challenges he faced in implementing the Aadhaar initiative within the Congress. This is an essential quality of a sherpa for Amrit Kaal initiatives, as similar challenges are bound to crop up for any new initiative undertaken.

Nilekani's urgency in issuing the first Aadhaar number to Ranjana Sonawane was a bold move that sent a strong message to naysayers. It showed that the Aadhaar initiative was not a pipe dream, but a real possibility. This step heralded Aadhaar as a reality and helped to build momentum for the initiative.[18]

He then picked up the pace of enrolment for Aadhaar by accelerating rapidly, from 100 million Aadhaar holders in November 2011 to 200 million by February 2012. This rapid growth caught many people by surprise, including those in the political and bureaucratic establishments.[19]

Later, in an interview to *Forbes India*, Nilekani revealed the thinking behind the meteoric rising in registration: 'We felt speed was strategic. Doing and scaling things quickly was critical. If you move very quickly it doesn't give opposition the time to consolidate.'

Despite facing challenges from various angles, the Aadhaar pivotal initiative continued to make progress, demonstrating its potential impact and the commitment of the sherpa in its development. Nilekani and his team remained focused on building a critical mass by enrolling at least 600 million Indians into the Aadhaar system. By early March 2014, half of India's 1.2 billion population had received their Aadhaar IDs on schedule.[20]

AS THE 2014 elections approached, the Aadhaar programme faced uncertainty. While its legal fate awaited the Supreme Court's decision, its future also hinged on the election outcome, raising questions about its continuation if the supporting government changed.[21]

As expected by several pollsters, the BJP won a majority in the Lok Sabha in the May 2014 general election in the lower house of the Indian Parliament, the Lok Sabha. This led to the formation of a new government led by Narendra Modi.

Prior to becoming Prime Minister, Narendra Modi had expressed concerns about the Aadhaar project. This led some observers to anticipate a potential slowdown or even a halt of the initiative after his election.

In the days leading up to Prime Minister Modi's public endorsement of Aadhaar, Nandan Nilekani met the PM and Finance Minister Arun Jaitley. Although the nature and details of their discussions remain undisclosed, the shift in position of Modi potentially stemmed from his apparent appreciation of the potential benefits of the programme such as improved efficiency in government services, reduced fraud and wider financial inclusion.[22]

AADHAAR EXEMPLIFIES how a pivotal initiative can transcend political shifts in a democratic system. While the initial steps toward a national ID system began under the BJP in the early 2000s, it was formally launched and completed by the subsequent Congress-led government. Since 2014, the newly elected BJP-led government has not only continued the initiative, but has expanded its scope manifold.

Nandan Nilekani resigned from UIDAI on 13 March 2014, but Aadhaar as a pivotal initiative had by then been successfully completed, and a firm framework had been laid for the world's largest biometric ID system.[23]

Following elections in May 2014, the newly formed Indian government led by Prime Minister Narendra Modi confirmed the expansion and legislative reinforcement of the Aadhaar programme. The government sought to leverage Aadhaar's biometric identification system to streamline service delivery and combat corruption. Citizen enrolment in the programme steadily increased.

However, the initiative faced opposition from privacy advocates and political groups, who raised concerns about potential infringements on individual liberties.

The Modi government demonstrated comprehensive engagement with the Aadhaar initiative, leveraging its significant potential while also being mindful of the anticipated opposition.

Aware of the likely challenges in securing smooth passage of the Aadhaar Bill through the Rajya Sabha due to a lack of majority, the government astutely introduced it as a money bill. This strategic move circumvented the need for Rajya Sabha approval, leveraging the government's majority in the Lok Sabha to enact the legislation. The Aadhaar (Targeted Delivery of Financial and Other Subsidies, Benefits and Services) Act of 2016 was thus adeptly passed as a Money Bill, marking a pivotal moment in the governance of Aadhaar.[24]

This legislation firmly established the framework governing Aadhaar, detailing its objectives, the authority of the UIDAI and the conditions under which Aadhaar could be utilised.

The approach taken by the current government in transforming an implemented pivotal initiative into a legal framework might work as a template for pivotal initiatives undertaken during Amrit Kaal.

Furthermore, the bill uniquely positioned the UIDAI as the sole agency entrusted to issue Aadhaar numbers, mandating enrolment for all Indian citizens. It expanded the government's capacity to utilise Aadhaar numbers across a broad spectrum, including the distribution of subsidies, benefits and services. This functionality emerged as a key factor in the government's evolving perspective on Aadhaar, recognising it as an instrumental tool for enhancing the efficiency and integrity of government programmes. The Bill also provided for the protection of the privacy of Aadhaar data.

In 2016, the government formalised the procedures for enrolling for Aadhaar and updating the information in an Aadhaar card. In addition, the regulations for setting out the procedures for authenticating an Aadhaar number and the use of Aadhaar for electronic authentication were finalised.[25]

The government showed urgency in widening the scope of Aadhaar and passed the Finance Act 2017, which became a major piece of legislation that had a significant impact on the Indian economy. Under this act, Aadhaar became mandatory for filing income tax returns. In addition, it became mandatory for banks and financial institutions to collect Aadhaar numbers from their customers for the purpose of identification and verification.[26]

In 2017, the government came out with the National Policy on Electronics. It recognised the importance of Aadhaar as a key enabler for digital transformation in India. The policy acknowledged that Aadhaar can be used to enable secure and convenient electronic transactions and to improve the efficiency of government services. This was in line with the government's vision to promote digitisation and ease of doing business in India. The policy also emphasised the need to ensure the privacy and security of Aadhaar data and to promote the use of indigenous technologies in its implementation.

Following four years of experience with Aadhaar, the government introduced the Aadhaar Amendment Act in 2019. This amendment permitted the issuing of Aadhaar numbers to children, potentially facilitating access to services and benefits from an early age. This also mandated telecom companies to verify the identity of their subscribers using Aadhaar, aiming to enhance security and prevent misuse.[27]

AT THE same time, the government also actively formed new policies around Aadhaar. The National Digital Identity Policy released in 2018 sets out a clear vision for the use of Aadhaar in India. It highlights the importance of Aadhaar in improving public service delivery, reducing fraud and promoting financial inclusion. The policy also emphasised the need to protect the privacy and security of Aadhaar data and to ensure that its use is in compliance with the law.[28]

The success of another pivotal initiative, the PMJDY—that was designed to promote financial inclusion—could possibly be attributed to the Aadhaar initiative. Aadhaar IDs played a crucial role in verifying the identity of citizens for this programme, enabling the opening of bank accounts for millions. This has helped millions of Indians, especially those from low-income households, to access banking services and avail various government schemes and subsidies.

The Pradhan Mantri Kaushal Vikas Yojana (PMKVY) is another great initiative introduced by the government to promote skill development among Indian youth. Aadhaar plays a key role in this programme by verifying the identity of trainees and tracking their progress. This helps in ensuring transparency and accountability in the training process and helps trainees to avail various benefits and subsidies provided by the government. Overall, PMKVY is a great step towards empowering the youth of India and enhancing their employability.

AADHAAR MIGHT have been, by far, the most successful pivotal initiative in India since the country's birth and unification as a nation state in August 1947. What is remarkable is that it survived challenges and criticism, both in society and in the Indian political and court systems.

Aadhaar is now the world's largest biometric identity programme, covering about 16 per cent of the world's population. Over 1.38 billion Aadhaar numbers have been issued and more than 80 million daily usages testify to the success of the original concept of the initiative.[29]

The success of Aadhaar is a testament to the idea of designing an initiative for addressing a crisis. It demonstrates the enormous importance of the team leader, Nandan Nilekani. He was instrumental in overcoming the challenges that Aadhaar faced and in making it a success.

The Indian Government is actively promoting Aadhaar as a foundation for transformative initiatives aimed at improving citizen services. For secure and efficient travel, Aadhaar-enabled e-passports will significantly enhance document security, streamline the passport process and minimise the risk of fraud and misuse.

The current government is already working on various new initiatives that will use Aadhaar as a bedrock. One such initiative that is particularly exciting is Aadhaar-enabled healthcare, where Aadhaar could be used to improve healthcare delivery. Aadhaar can be used to track patients' medical records, to verify the identity of healthcare providers and to make payments for healthcare services. The government is also planning to use Aadhaar to improve the delivery of social welfare schemes. Aadhaar can be used to verify the identities of beneficiaries, track deliveries of benefits and to prevent fraud.

The central lesson to be learnt here is about the need to understand the imperative for and to design a pivotal initiative, allow a committed and visionary leader to implement it and then support it through Parliamentary laws, Acts, regulations and newer complementary initiatives.

'THE SUCCESS of India's digital public infrastructure and technologies such as Aadhaar, UPI, Co-Win and Pradhan Mantri Jan Dhan Yojana have effectively delivered services directly to beneficiaries. India has shown that technology can be a big enabler of ensuring last-mile delivery. Technology has helped India achieve targeted welfare delivery,' Modi said on 26 August 2023 in an exclusive interview with *India Today*.[30]

***

Financial Inclusion of the Bottom of the Pyramid

Pradhan Mantri Jan Dhan Yojana

It is a 'significant milestone' that the flagship scheme for financial inclusion—Pradhan Mantri Jan Dhan Yojana—has crossed 500 million, with 56 per cent of bank accounts belonging to women and 67 per cent of those opened in rural and semi-urban areas.

—**Prime Minister Narendra Modi**
20 August 2023[1]

ON 15 August 2014, in his Independence Day address to the nation from the historic grounds of the Red Fort in New Delhi, the newly elected Prime Minister Narendra Modi declared a pivotal initiative: to launch the world's largest financial inclusion programme.

This programme, named PMJDY, aimed to transform the lives of millions by bringing them into the formal banking system. This decision marked a crucial moment in India's economic landscape, paving the way for greater financial empowerment and inclusivity for the previously unbanked segments of Indian society.

In his trademark style, Modi laid a compelling case for his flagship initiative in his speech. However, most citizens living in India, or those living abroad but watching the 'first act of a new prime minister,' had doubts whether this initiative was destined to become another catchy slogan, just like *Garibi Hatao Desh Bachao* of 1971.[2] It's unclear if Modi truly grasped the deep concerns of citizens at large about the initiative's effectiveness, given the long history of similar well-meaning plans that have failed to deliver on their promises since Independence.

In an effort to promote social and economic equality, the Indian Government under Prime Minister Indira Gandhi nationalised 14 major commercial banks on 19 July 1969. These banks, which included industry leaders such as Bank of Baroda and Punjab National Bank, controlled an estimated 70 per cent of the country's banking assets. This move, a hallmark of Gandhi's socialist policies, aimed to increase access to credit for small businesses and farmers, who were often underserved by the private banking sector.[3]

It is a fact that several prime ministers from time to time, either from the Red Fort or during election rallies, had made promises of implementing similar impressive programmes for reducing the suffering of the poor. However, for one reason or another, rarely any perceptible results were seen on the ground.

As Modi, on 15 August 2014, was well and truly within the 'political honeymoon period', most citizens perceived the PMJDY as a 'government programme' and not as a reachable destination within the timeframe outlined by him in his speech.

Many perhaps believed that Modi wanted to project himself as a different leader from the past, particularly when seen in the light of the long and effective election campaign he ran, leading to his astonishing victory. Citizens of the country were willing to accept the PMJDY as a nice plan, but one that would ultimately lead to limited success.[4]

Several World Bank studies had reported that financial inclusion is a building block for both poverty reduction and opportunities for economic growth. The World Bank Group, with private and public sector partners, set an ambitious target to achieve Universal Financial Access by 2020.[5]

Modi, in his speech that Independence Day, came across as someone who has 'read' these research notes in detail, particularly when he expressed a good grasp of the crisis in India.

In this speech, Modi said that when any poor family faces a financial emergency, they have nowhere to go but to unscrupulous moneylenders who charge them 10 times the interest of a bank. This traps them in a perpetual cycle of debt where the poor can afford to barely pay the exuberant interest and is never able to reduce the loan amount. This traps the poor in an endless cycle forever.[6]

Modi might well have been talking about Ramesh Babu, a bangle-maker of Andhra Pradesh who was paying 10 per cent interest on his Rs 30,000 loan to a local moneylender, and was only able to repay the interest amount. This crisis led Ramesh to contemplate suicide.[7]

'I wish to connect the poorest citizens of the country with the facility of bank accounts,' said Modi.

Modi showed an even deeper understanding of the crisis again in his 28 August 2014 address at the time of the formal launch of the initiative. He said, 'Indian women have shown their deep-rooted habit of working hard and saving money. But their struggle and frustration are with their menfolk. A typical poor woman tries to hide her hard-earned money in tin boxes or inside the utensils so that her husband (who is often lazy and has the bad habit of drinking) doesn't steal her money to satisfy his desire.'

With his flagship initiative, Modi said he wanted to end the misery of women by bringing them into a formal financial system with bank accounts in their names. He sounded confident that it would help solve this problem among countless others.[8]

THE AMBITIOUS financial inclusion initiative launched by Prime Minister Modi in August 2014 faced significant challenges from the outset. While the scheduled launch date of 28 August 2014 signalled a sense of urgency, several key government departments struggled to translate the policy into an effective actionable idea.

A major hurdle was the lack of enthusiastic participation from the Indian bureaucracy. Often referred to as 'recalcitrant,' many government departments may have been resistant to change for various reasons. Bureaucratic systems have been slow to adapt and to implement a large-scale initiative such as PMJDY and would have required significant adjustments to existing workflows and procedures. Reaching a large, often dispersed, population would have required significant investment in expanding internet connectivity and access to digital tools in rural areas.

The crisis of 'putting bureaucracy to work' was confirmed as far back as 2010 by the widely regarded Hong Kong-based group, Political and Economic Risk Consultancy, when they concluded that India's bureaucratic system is one of the most stifling in the world. What is interesting is that this study also confirmed a strong link between the bureaucracy and corruption. Finally, it established a widely held belief that Indian bureaucrats are selfish and highly insensitive to the needs of the people they are supposed to help.[9]

Barack Obama, perhaps, was spot on in his widely read book titled *A Promised Land* when he squarely put the blame on the whims of corrupt local officials and power brokers, hamstrung by a parochial bureaucracy that was resistant to change.[10]

During the previous 10 years of the UPA regime, the productivity of the bureaucracy had slid even lower when it became too emotionally disconnected, intellectually unconvinced and professionally inefficient for the administration and implementation of new programmes.[11]

Several key people doubted Modi's ambitious programme. The person with whom the buck was supposed to stop—the RBI governor, Raghuram Rajan—had publicly warned the banks not to run after records. 'We have to make sure the Jan Dhan Yojana does not go off track,' he had said at a conference on 1 September 2014. 'The target is universality, not just speed and numbers.'[12]

The second dimension of the crisis was the size of the unbanked population in India. World Bank data from 2011 revealed a low baseline for financial inclusion in India, with only 35 per cent of the population having access to a formal financial account (bank or other regulated institution).[13]

In other words, 65 per cent were part of what Modi called 'financial untouchability'—the ones being targeted by Modi's initiative for lifting out of poverty.

The third strand of the crisis was wide variations of the account holders across the country—from 62.2 per cent in the southern region to 28.6 per cent in the eastern region.[14]

The fourth strand was one that emerged as a chorus of criticism from thought leaders, including M S Sriram, visiting faculty at the Centre for Public Policy at the Indian Institute of Management in Bangalore. Sriram argued that the PMJDY needed to go beyond simply opening accounts.

'The state needs to put its resources to ensure that the infrastructure backbone is available—which means that there is ubiquitous presence of interoperable point of sale devices that allow people to transact without a hefty fee...Once this architecture is available, the poor will start transacting.'[15]

HOWEVER, MODI seemed to believe in what Carl Friedrich said; 'Public policy, to put it flatly, is a continuous process, the formulation of which is inseparable from its execution.'[16]

As a result, from the word go, he squarely remained in focus of the execution of his pivotal initiative and potentially ignored the noise from various 'experts,' some of whom were supposed to be 'inside the tent.'

In that sense, Modi might have taken a leaf out of Brazilian President Lula who was of the opinion that the experts and academics know very little about the poor.[17]

MODI, PERHAPS, also tried to take advantage of his position as a newly minted PM and set an ambitious target for the formal launch of the initiative. In doing so, he challenged the bureaucracy to overcome their tendency to create hurdles for nearly every policy in India, just like in the past.

He directly challenged two of the worst-performing public institutions—banks and insurance houses in India. In hindsight, this could be seen as tactics for taking the recalcitrant bureaucratic system in India head-on and set the tone for his full term as PM.

A senior bank employee with 19 years of experience shared that their team worked over the weekend for the first time ever. This unprecedented effort reflects the immense pressure that was placed on bank employees nationwide to meet the ambitious PMJDY target of 10 million new accounts on its launch day.[18] Throughout the country, every branch and its staff worked literally day and night to meet the target.

To facilitate this ambitious target, some 600 programmes and 77,852 camps were held across India for the opening of bank accounts. This was a massive undertaking and helped to ensure that the PMJDY got off to a strong start.[19] The Guinness Book of World Records confirmed this achievement, stating: 'The most bank accounts opened in one week as a part of a financial inclusion campaign is 18,096,130 and was achieved by the Government of India from August 23 to 29, 2014.'[20]

Modi played the 'good-cop-bad cop' role well. He reportedly wrote to 7,000 banking leaders underlining how important the initiative was and asked for their full cooperation for the roll-out of the initiative to its ultimate target. On 28 August 2014, when the initiative was formally launched, he first congratulated everyone in achieving the target of 15 million accounts.

What was more important was that, as he stressed, the

achievement had driven a key point home—if a target is set, the Indian bureaucratic system can achieve it. He added that this achievement will provide confidence to the entire bureaucracy for achieving any future targets. Appreciating efforts by everyone at critical stages of an initiative is an important lesson for Amrit Kaal.

Clearly, Modi was able to nudge what Obama called the parochial bureaucracy to change its approach and work tirelessly to implement the initial target of the pivotal initiative.

WITH A flying start to his first pivotal initiative, Modi brought in his sherpa to take the resolve further to its logical conclusion.

Dr Hasmukh Adhia, a 1981-batch IAS officer, became the Union financial services secretary initially and then later the revenue secretary, to resolve the nuts and bolts of the initiative. He had earned the confidence and respect of Modi, as he worked with him in Gujarat when he was the chief minister.

Acknowledging the significance of the PMJDY as a flagship initiative for financial inclusion, Dr Adhia demonstrably took swift action to expand its reach. Recognising it as the new government's first major announcement, he adopted a proactive approach, aiming to widen the programme's scope from the very beginning.

Dr Adhia came up with an innovative plan to achieve 100 per cent financial inclusion under the PMJDY scheme. He called it the 'Open Challenge Mode,' whereby any citizen of the country that so far had been excluded from having a bank account could simply walk into a bank and demand to open an account. All banks had been obligated to open an account for them on the spot, thereby doing away with all barriers and the insistence on necessary checks and balances.[21]

An important learning for designing new initiatives for

Amrit Kaal is that all the shortcomings of past efforts by previous governments should be taken into account and innovative solutions should be found to plug those gaps.

The second obstacle that threatened to derail the process was the limited availability of physical bank branches in rural India. This, perhaps, stemmed from the historical focus on urban areas following bank nationalisation in 1969. As a result, a significant portion of the rural population was excluded from crucial financial services.[22]

Dr Adhia anticipated this challenge early on and offered a workaround immediately for rural India's financial inclusion. It was decided not to wait for physical branch expansion in rural areas, but rather engage retail agents as Business Correspondents (BCs).[23]

These BCs ended up acting as an extended arm of the banks, offering basic banking services in locations far beyond the range of brick-and-mortar branches. This enabled the PMJDY to reach remote areas at a lower cost compared to establishing new branches. Additionally, BCs often belonged to the local communities they served, fostering trust and credibility among the community members.

Dr Adhia focused on process simplification and customer convenience as a core of the PMJDY initiative.[24]

As a starter, the account opening form was reduced to one page that was simple and universal right across the country. At the same time, the use of e-KYC reduced paperwork and documentation. The entire account opening process was completed quickly and the accounts were instantly activated.

Second, the working hours for opening new accounts were extended, which enabled more women to open accounts.

Third, a conscious decision was made to bundle multiple services into a single product. As a result, new bank accounts came with a RuPay Card, mobile banking, insurance and a credit overdraft facility.

Finally, resolution of issues was completed through various options—email, toll free number, portal and physical letters. There were strict timeframes for attending to a grievance (2 days) and for resolving it (5–7 days).

With regard to the success in opening new accounts, Raghuram Rajan, the then RBI Governor, agreed with the need and progress of the initiative, saying that he was not worried about the quality of the KYC for opening new accounts and welcomed the financial inclusion scheme. 'We welcome the Jan Dhan Yojana; it is part of RBI's plan to get universal access.'[25]

The efforts of the sherpa and the banking and insurance managers produced stellar results—by the end, every household had at least one bank account.

On 28 August 2014, Modi referred to the contribution of the insurance sector by saying it might be the first time in the history of the insurance sector that so many new covers were granted.

The initiative was designed comprehensively with a built-in feedback loop for accessing the deposit and debit history of account holders. This enabled the initiative to roll out the second phase that included a RuPay debit card. Access to an overdraft facility was also granted as part of this. The objective of this phase was to get the poor out of the clutches of unscrupulous money lenders.

By 4 November 2020, there were 302 million RuPay cards and 412 million Jan Dhan accounts (PMJDY accounts), a great achievement by any yardstick, though the smaller number of RuPay cards relative to Jan Dhan accounts was a cause of concern. [26]

Another feature of this initiative, which perhaps has a key lesson for Amrit Kaal, was that newly banked citizens were not left out in the cold, but were provided with an opportunity to become financially literate. Some of the learnings included how to develop a regular saving habit, how to use an ATM safely, how to avail of insurance and pensions and how to use basic mobile phones for banking services.

LIKE WITH everything else in life, things do not always go as planned.

A large number of Jan Dhan accounts were found to have zero account balance and these were threatening to undo all the hard work that had gone into opening an account. According to data released by the ministry, only 28 per cent of the accounts opened under the scheme are currently active, with about Rs 9,000 crore deposited in them.[27]

The zero balance accounts potentially indicated limited disposable income among account holders. In addition, the public sector banks and insurance companies were worried about the cost of servicing these accounts eating into their net profits.[28]

Another lesson for Amrit Kaal initiatives can be found here: That one should look beyond setbacks; embrace adaptability and innovate!

The PMJDY implementing team started to brainstorm ways to undo the zero-balance situation. The obvious choice was that all government welfare schemes should switch to the direct benefit transfer (DBT) mode. There were 59 central government schemes and the government now started transferring money directly to beneficiary accounts.[29]

The direct benefit transfer step helped with the declining number of zero-balance accounts significantly, with the number falling below 25 per cent on 5 February 2017. This achievement marks a major milestone for the initiative with measurable effectiveness in achieving financial inclusion.[30]

PMJDY IS Prime Minister Narendra Modi's first social upliftment initiative. No wonder Modi has consistently referred to it as a major achievement in four of his Independence Day speeches since assuming office. The government's flagship financial inclusion drive, by virtue of its sheer scale, is one of the grandest policy initiatives of its kind.[31]

'As we mark nine years of PM Jan Dhan Yojana, I congratulate all those who benefited from this scheme and laud everyone who worked to make it a success. It is a milestone effort in empowering our people,' Modi said in a post on X on 29 August 2023. 'Through this initiative, we have brought millions into the financial mainstream, ensuring every Indian has a rightful place in our growing economy.'[32]

The PMJDY reached a new milestone on 21 August 2023, almost nine years after its launch, by exceeding 500 million bank accounts. What is significant is that 56 per cent of those accounts belong to women and 67 per cent of them were opened in rural and semi-urban areas.[33]

There are ongoing challenges with the PMJDY that are being addressed with new initiatives. While PMJDY accounts have provided access to financial services to many women, limited utilisation beyond cashing-out benefits presents a challenge.

New innovative approaches have been designed and implemented by some banks with a focus on encouraging broader financial engagement beyond basic transactions that could unlock the full potential of the initiative.

Bank of Baroda rolled out Jan Dhan Plus for encouraging

low-income women to save regularly in their Jan Dhan accounts. Early results are positive and similar accounts are being rolled out to rural areas.[34]

At the same time, the government is committed to building on the success of the initiative. The government has built a new pivotal initiative called the Jan Dhan Aadhaar Mobile (JAM) Trinity, by linking the Jan Dhan bank account, the Aadhaar unique identity number and the beneficiary's mobile phone number, allowing benefits to be transferred directly to the verified bank accounts of identified beneficiaries in a much more transparent manner.[35]

THE PRESIDENT of India, Droupadi Murmu, in her address to the joint sitting of the Lok Sabha and the Rajya Sabha in the Parliament on 31 January 2024 summed up the impact of this successful pivotal initiative: 'The trinity of Jan Dhan Aadhaar Mobile (JAM) has helped curb corruption. My government has so far transferred Rs 34 lakh crore through DBT [direct benefit transfer]. Thanks to the Jan Dhan Aadhaar Mobile (JAM), about 10 crore fake beneficiaries have been weeded out from the system. This has helped prevent Rs 2.75 lakh crore from going into wrong hands.' (President of India, Address to Parliament, 31 January 2024).[36]

***

Ushering in Behavioural Change among Billions

Swachh Bharat Abhiyan

I don't know if people will appreciate my talking about dirt and toilets from the Red Fort but I come from a poor family. I have seen poverty and the attempt to give dignity to the poor starts from there.

—Prime Minister Narendra Modi
Independence Day Speech, 15 August 2014[1]

A clean India would be the best tribute India could pay to Mahatma Gandhi on his 150th birth anniversary in 2019.

—Prime Minister Narendra Modi
Speech at the launch of the
Swachh Bharat Abhiyan, 2 October 2014[2]

IN HIS maiden Independence Day speech from the ramparts of the majestic Red Fort on 15 August 2014, the newly elected Prime Minister of India astonished everyone, particularly when seen with the backdrop of his election promise of *Achhe din aane waale hain* (Better days are on the way). In a first for any head of state in India, Modi acknowledged publicly the deep crisis of open defecation in the country and gave a clarion call to end it in the next five years.[3]

Several listeners, who had grown used to tall promises year after year in Independence Day speeches, viewed it as another *jumla*—a colloquial term for a false promise by a politician.

But Modi dedicated a good part of his speech on the issue, and in doing so, he demonstrated a deep understanding of the sanitation crisis India had faced up to that time. He acknowledged the shameful reality that nearly half the population, 55 crore people, primarily in rural areas, lacked access to basic toilet facilities. This staggering statistic, coupled with the nationally low sanitation coverage of just 39 per cent, painted a grim picture of a mammoth challenge demanding immediate and decisive action.

Beyond the numbers, Prime Minister Modi recognised the far-reaching consequences of this crisis. Open defecation not only posed a threat to public health, but also impacted individual dignity and safety, particularly of women and girls. It resonated with him as a barrier to India's social and economic progress.

Studies have consistently shown that inadequate sanitation and open defecation have severe negative consequences for the wellbeing of citizens, especially the poor and young children. Not only does it directly and undeniably impact people's dignity and safety—women and girls, in particular, face a higher risk of harassment and assault when they lack access to safe sanitation facilities, but it is also a major cause for the spread of infectious diseases such as diarrhoea, cholera, and intestinal infections. These diseases can lead to malnutrition, stunting in children and even death.[4]

Further, it exacerbates environmental degradation, particularly of water resources. Contaminated water from open defecation pollutes groundwater and rivers, making it unsafe for drinking and irrigation.[5]

International organisations such as the World Bank have emphasised the devastating effects of poor sanitation and hygiene on overall progress, particularly economic development in terms of loss of productivity due to illness and the high costs of treating sanitation-related diseases.[6]

The World Bank estimated the value of the impact of inadequate sanitation in India as equal to US $53 billion (Rs 240 lakh crore) in the year 2006, equivalent to 6.4 per cent of India's GDP in the same year.[7] With population increase and the consequential deterioration of sanitation, its impact would have increased manifold since 2006.

IT HAS been reported that economic impact has several facets. On the one hand, poor sanitation increases health care costs and directly results in loss of productivity of workers, and on the other hand, children who are sick are more likely to miss school, which leads to lower educational attainment and a negative impact on their future economic prospects. [8]

Perhaps the most frightening impact is on the future generation. India ranks among the countries with the worst undernutrition, stunting and wasting levels in the world, even worse than some countries in sub-Saharan Africa. These conditions can have a devastating impact on children's physical and cognitive development.[9]

It has been estimated by various research groups that about 40 per cent of our children were stunted. The long-term effects of undernutrition can be devastating. Children who are stunted are more likely to have lower IQs, shorter stature and an increased risk of chronic diseases such as heart disease, stroke and diabetes. They are also more likely to be unemployed and earn lower incomes as adults.[10]

Poor sanitation also has a number of indirect costs such as the loss of tourism revenue and the damage to a country's reputation.[11] The study analysed the evidence with respect to the adverse economic impacts of inadequate sanitation, including the costs associated with death and disease, accessing and treating water as well as losses in education, productivity, time and tourism.

Even Modi may have underestimated the scale of the crisis. UNICEF in 2015 reported nearly half of India's population—around 568 million people—suffered the indignity of defecating in fields, forests, bodies of water or other public spaces, including along railway tracks, due to a lack of access to toilets. India alone accounted for 90 per cent of the people in South Asia and half of the 1.2 billion people in the world that defecated in the open.[12]

THE OPEN defecation crisis did not grow to a humungous proportion overnight. Like many other crises that India faced since Independence, India tried to kick the sanitation crisis 'into the long grass' for a long time.

Despite efforts by the Indian Government and by volunteer

organisations, attempts to improve sanitation have been largely unsuccessful. Committees and commissions, such as the Malkani Committee established in 1961, failed to produce concrete, practical solutions tailored to local needs. These initiatives ultimately amounted to little more than superficial gestures.[13]

Many readers might be surprised to learn that India's government only began allocating funds for sanitation 40 years after Independence. The Central Rural Sanitation Programme (CRSP), launched in 1986, marked India's first nationwide initiative to improve rural sanitation. This programme aimed to enhance the quality of life for rural communities and, more importantly, address issues of privacy and dignity for women.[14]

The CRSP aimed to provide proper sanitation facilities to at least 25 per cent of the rural population by the end of the 1980s. However, the programme primarily focused on building toilets, taking a supply-driven approach rather than fostering long-term behaviour change.[15]

In the early 1990s, the Indian Government realised the failure of the CRSP and rebranded it as the Total Sanitation Campaign (TSC) in 1999. The newly named programme rightly had greater emphasis on changing behaviour and generating demand for toilets. With the aim to make India open defecation-free (ODF) by 2017, the campaign dispersed information, education and communication materials about the health consequences of open defecation.[16]

After 30 years of the first budget allocation and lofty aspiration of the TSC, India still had 568 million people suffering the indignity of defecating in the open in 2014. Clearly, the successive governments' efforts had failed miserably.

It's not as if policymakers were not aware of the main issue. 'We need a cultural revolution in this country to completely change people's attitudes toward sanitation and hygiene,' said Jairam Ramesh, an economist and former sanitation minister in 2011.

It was perhaps the first time the main issue of attitudinal change was debated widely. Indians have held a habit of defecating in the open for centuries due to 'beliefs, values and norms about purity.' Many considered open defecation as 'promoting purity and strength, particularly of male bodies' and so it was considered a socially acceptable, healthy activity, especially in rural areas.[17]

The UPA government decided to form a new Ministry of Drinking Water and Sanitation (MDWS) that was mandated to tackle the problem and usher in behavioural change in citizens.[18] This approach was similar to what many governments worldwide had previously taken—throw resources at the problem and hope for significant progress through sheer bureaucratic volume.

MDWS launched a rather narrowly focused subsidised programme that exclusively took up the idea of toilet construction.[19] In the same year, the Bill & Melinda Gates Foundation launched the 'Reinvent the Toilet Challenge' to provide a much-needed awareness campaign.[20]

All genuine efforts by successive governments and charity foundations failed to make a difference in the problem.

What came out loud and clear was that 'throwing money' at an issue rarely yields the desired result, and that a real problem can only be solved by launching a pivotal initiative, with comprehensive understanding of the crisis and a dogged determination to implement it until visible results are seen on the ground.

MODI HAD been Chief Minister of Gujarat for 12 years before becoming Prime Minister and during that time, he had overseen several successful sanitation initiatives in the state. He also had a personal interest in the issue, as he had grown up in a village where open defecation was common.

Modi had understood the problem and seemed determined to ignite a national movement to take the issue of open defection head-on. He announced the launch of a pivotal initiative that he called the Swachh Bharat Mission (SBM).[21]

HAVING AN accurate sense of the crisis is a good place to start. And Modi knew, and rightly so, that the government and its machinery, including bureaucrats, could not make even a dent in the crisis unless he thought outside the box (Iyer 2019).

Modi adopted a distinctive strategy compared to the feeble governmental endeavours earlier on the issue. During the launch of the pivotal initiative, he astutely connected the situation to Mahatma Gandhi. In his speech, Modi said, 'There were two things extremely close to Mahatma Gandhi's heart—the Independence of India and sanitation. But, given a choice, he had said that sanitation was even more important than political independence' (Iyer 2019).

He then put the onus on his government and its bureaucrats as well as on the citizens of the country. Involving the stakeholders in the initiative was the key aspect that distinguished his approach from the earlier attempts. He asked pointedly, 'Can we resolve that in 2019, when we celebrate Mahatma Gandhi's 150th birth anniversary, our village, our city, our street, our community, our school, our temple, our hospital, and all areas will be free from dirt and filth?'[22]

AFTER TWO months of preparation, Prime Minister Narendra Modi launched the SBM on 2 October 2014. This was the country's biggest-ever cleanliness drive, estimated to cost over Rs 62,000 crores. Modi emphasised that the mission is 'beyond politics' and is inspired by patriotism.[23]

This pivotal initiative aimed to make India cleaner and achieve universal sanitation coverage. He, thus, brought back the focus on sanitation.[24]

FROM THE outset, he embarked on a process of nationwide citizen engagement, aiming to create a movement beyond a government programme but one that had to be implemented through the existing bureaucratic channels. He touched the people with his sincerity when he declared that success wouldn't be achieved solely through government initiatives, but would require the active participation of the people. Therefore, he emphasised on the collective responsibility of undertaking this task together.

Prime Minister Modi's commitment to public participation in the SBM was evident in the programme's crowd-sourced logo contest. This approach, possibly the first of its kind in India, aimed to engage citizens from the outset of the programme. The winning logo featured Mahatma Gandhi's iconic spectacles. Announcing the winner, Modi said that the logo will remind all of us that Gandhi is continuously watching us and asking the pointed question, 'When are you making India clean?'[25]

So far, successive governments had given only limited prioritisation to sanitation. Other issues, often deemed more politically attractive than sanitation, often made it difficult to secure the necessary funding and resources.

To address this challenge, the Modi government came out with an innovative model that should be used for new initiatives leading up to Amrit Kaal. US $20 million was allocated under shared funding between the central and state governments, but the latter were allowed more autonomy in managing it.

This pivotal initiative produced astonishing results due to the decentralised decision-making approach taken right from the start. It empowered state governments to decide the most effective modality for further decentralising funding down to the household level, encouraging local ownership and tailoring solutions to specific regional needs. This enabled appropriate public financing and efficient roll-out of an initiative with joint funding from both the state and central governments. As a result, the initiative was treated as everyone's business.[26]

HOWEVER, THE astonishing success of this pivotal initiative would not have been possible without a dedicated sherpa. The challenge demanded a new breed of leadership—one with not only sanitation expertise, but also the vision and creativity to trigger a large-scale behavioural shift in over a billion people.

The sherpa was Parameswaran Iyer (Param), who put his hand up to work on the initiative while still leading a crucial water and sanitation project for the World Bank in Vietnam. This could be taken as a good omen for the success of the initiative because, as the sherpa, he had hands on experience in this area.

Param, a graduate of St Stephen's College, New Delhi, had served in the Indian Administrative Services for over twenty-three years, holding senior management positions across both the Government of India and the state of Uttar Pradesh. However, his most critical asset for the role of SBM's sherpa was the expertise in water and sanitation gained during his fifteen years with the World Bank, where he worked on projects in Bangladesh, Sri Lanka, Vietnam, China, Egypt and Lebanon.[27]

Param was in Hanoi, Vietnam, when Modi was walking to the ramparts of the Red Ford in New Delhi for his maiden address to the nation on 15 August 2014, and he was curious to know the vision of the newly elected prime minister for India's progress and growth. But Prime Minister Modi's passionate speech about the lack of toilets in India and its impact on dignity, particularly for women and girls, jolted Param. He could hardly believe the newly minted PM's focus on open defecation and his intention to eradicate it through the SBM. Param reportedly turned to his wife and said he needed to get back to India and somehow get involved in the SBM.

In 2016, after resigning from the World Bank, he was appointed secretary to the Government of India in the Ministry of Drinking Water and Sanitation in New Delhi. From 2016 to 2020, he was the sherpa for the implementation of India's ambitious US $20 billion SBM.[28]

Param's case is unique. Like a sherpa, he proactively volunteered his expertise and passion, which led the government to recognise his potential and appoint him as the pointsman for the initiative.

ONE OF the major hurdles to improving sanitation in India is its vast and decentralised landscape. With over 600,000 villages, each with its unique needs and challenges, implementing a one-size-fits-all solution proves difficult.

Upon joining the ministry, Param confronted the twin behemoths: building sanitation infrastructure and changing ingrained social behaviours. He likened it to the daunting task of 'painting the wings of a plane in flight'. Further, he identified a lack of inherent demand for toilets due to deeply entrenched centuries-old open defecation practices. This compounded the challenge.

Param adopted a novel approach to traditional government work. Under his ministry, 'mission-mode' replaced time-bound procedures and hierarchies. He recruited young talent for agile planning, PR, communication, social media and rapid feedback loops with districts. Even the Ministry of Environment was revamped through toilet renovations.

Soon, a 'new normal' emerged within his ministry, with work hours extending from early morning to late evening. Saturday was renamed 'ODF Saturday,' where video conferences were held with district collectors and several 'Lunch and Learn' workshops were held with frequent field visits.

These disruptions involved the entire senior management of the ministry as well as of other branches of the Central Government, even captivating Bollywood stars! The Comptroller and Auditor General of India personally demonstrated the twin-pit design's waste conversion into usable compost on one such occasion in 2018 (Parameswaran Iyer 2019).

HOWEVER, HIS initial battle was overcoming the bureaucracy's jadedness towards yet another new plan from the new government. The second source of their despondency was the ambitious target of eliminating open defecation by the 150th birthday of Mahatma Gandhi in October 2019 set by none other than the prime minister.

To reinvigorate the spirits of the initially lukewarm

bureaucracy, Param established a manageable target at the initiative's outset—that of focusing on 100 flagship districts. This strategy aimed to mitigate scepticism about the programme's scale and demonstrate its feasibility.

The plan proved successful. With the declaration of 100 ODF districts, doubts among government employees abated significantly. A collective sense of accomplishment emerged, fostering the belief that it could be done.

The next step was getting district level officials motivated towards a common target. Three key strategies proved instrumental in fostering their emotional engagement and pride in achieving ODF villages. A cadre of 500 young professionals was deployed in most districts of the country. These individuals injected fresh ideas and energy into district operations. Social and mass media were leveraged strategically for facilitating public awareness and motivation, fostering a sense of collective responsibility. Finally, political leadership embodied new social norms, setting a powerful example for the public and district officials through their actions regarding cleanliness.[29]

The transformative SBM offers valuable lessons for shaping new initiatives in the Amrit Kaal era. Two crucial learnings include securing the active participation of bureaucrats who were tasked with implementing it and leveraging the power of the media for widespread messaging.

At the same time, quick and effective feedback at the district level was organised and therefore even Param's ministry adapted to a 'new normal' as office times changed from early morning to late evenings along with the ODF Saturday conferences with the district administration.

THIS INITIATIVE was a unique one where a detailed media campaign including social media was launched. This approach was targeted at overcoming the biggest hurdle—behavioural change.

For generations, a stigma was associated with having toilets within homes. Traditional beliefs also dictated that men should defecate outdoors, while women should use toilets cleaned by others. The SBM tackled these issues head-on with impactful campaigns featuring popular Bollywood celebrities such as Akshay Kumar, Amitabh Bachchan and Anushka Sharma. These well-recognised celebrities and others from the cricketing field became 'brand ambassadors' for the cause. For wider reach, people with broad appeal in their home states were also appointed brand ambassadors for regional areas.[30]

New media campaigns were launched strategically to keep the momentum of the initiative going. In 2017, the *Darwaza Band* campaign launched by Amitabh Bachchan became very popular, and was used across the country in different languages. In a tweet, he said 'we want India to progress and also the villages! *Darwaza Band* is a roadmap to my clean India. *Swachh* Bharat.'

Another innovative approach was taken to debunk the strongly held myth of the toilet-within-the-home premise. Bollywood literally rolled their sleeves up to tackle this one. Shree Narayan Singh made a movie called *Toilet Ek Prem Katha* that addressed the myth head-on.

PARAM'S MINISTRY leveraged available technologies to their full potential, playing a key role in the initiative's success. It showed how hundreds of thousands of implementers and community volunteers could be trained as part of the broader team.[31]

His ministry leveraged a comprehensive online management

information system (MIS) to track its progress in ending open defecation through toilet construction and use. The MIS captured household data from all *Gram Panchayats* (village councils) nationwide. State governments uploaded information based on this data, enabling the central, state, district and village levels to monitor individual household and community toilet construction.

The MIS went beyond construction tracking. It was upgraded to monitor the creation and sustainability of ODF communities. Additionally, an SMS system was used to verify toilet construction directly with beneficiaries through their mobile numbers.

Finally, a dedicated SBM dashboard provided visual progress reports with key performance indicators and interactive maps displaying nationwide programme progress.

THE SBM demonstrated the critical role of sustained engagement from top political leadership throughout the initiative's lifecycle. Prime Minister Modi consistently championed the programme all through its five-year duration, contributing to its success in several ways. For public recognition, he regularly used his *Mann Ki Baat* radio programme, to praise the efforts of individuals, departments and organisations involved in the mission.

He actively promoted the initiative and public participation through social media, even launching the '#MyCleanIndia' campaign to amplify public engagement and highlight the importance of cleanliness.

By consistently championing the initiative, recognising contributions and actively engaging the public, Prime Minister Modi as the leader provided crucial momentum and inspiration, contributing significantly to the success of the SBM.

The SBM stands as a powerful testament to the transformative potential of focused action and is a shining example of how rapid progress can be achieved, delivering a profound and immediate positive impact on the lives of millions. The success of the SBM hinged on a powerful combination of a dedicated sherpa and sustained support from the leadership at the highest levels. This was crucial for ensuring the initiative's long-term viability. Enlisting sustained public participation was critical for driving long-term behavioural change and fostering a sense of ownership among citizens (Iyer 2019).

It offers a perfect and effective template for new pivotal initiatives for the Amrit Kaal period.

CAPITALISING ON the momentum of the SBM's impressive achievements, the government swiftly launched its second phase on 1 October 2021. This decisive action positions SBM II as a prime example for initiatives undertaken during India's Amrit Kaal. The success of SBM Phase I serves as a valuable blueprint, paving the way for SBM II to tackle even more ambitious and challenging goals.

Christened the 'Swachh Bharat Mission-Urban 2.0 (SBM-U 2.0)' and 'AMRUT 2.0,' SBM-U II builds upon the success of the first phase and sets ambitious goals for India's rapidly urbanising landscape. Its core objectives are to make all cities 'garbage free' and 'water secure,' directly addressing critical sanitation and water management challenges. Ultimately, SBM-U 2.0 and AMRUT 2.0 aim to contribute significantly to the achievement of the United Nations' Sustainable Development Goals (SDGs) by 2030.[32]

To further solidify the gains from the SBM, efforts are underway to translate the initiative's core principles into a legal framework. A parliamentary panel recently debated and recommended a new law penalising public littering, including spitting, urinating and throwing garbage. This proposed legislation aims to provide legal teeth to the government's ambitious mission, fostering greater public compliance and propelling India towards a cleaner future.

In addition, the panel also advocated for introducing a chapter on the SBM programme in the primary school syllabus, to cultivate cleanliness habits in students.

The report's authors were of the firm opinion that merely bringing in behavioural change and self-regulation may not be sufficient and a central law to enforce the cleanliness drive would help.[33]

IMAGINE THE elation of all those who had borne the brunt of the seemingly Sisyphean task on the momentous day the Swachh Bharat Mission phase 2.0 was launched.

In his address after launching SBM-U 2.0 and AMRUT 2.0, Prime Minister Narendra Modi said, 'We have to remember that maintaining cleanliness is not just for a day, a fortnight, a year or for a few people; it is a mega campaign for every day, every fortnight, every year, for everyone and a continuous programme from one generation to another.'[34]

***

CONCLUSION

Yes, India Can
Roadmap for a Viksit Bharat

The best way to predict your future is to create it.

—Abraham Lincoln

We learn from history that we do not learn from history.

—G W F Hegel

DURING MY 21-day mandatory quarantine in China, a period enforced due to the COVID-19 pandemic while I was there to oversee our company's operations, I found myself contemplating a fundamental question about the responses of different nations to the unprecedented crisis. My curiosity was piqued by the contrasting approaches of China and India, two countries on divergent paths for handling the pandemic despite their respective growth narratives.

China, a country celebrated globally for its remarkable economic expansion over the past 25 years and often lauded for its comprehensive development, seemed to falter in its response to the COVID-19 crisis. This was intriguing, especially given its reputed efficiency and governance model. On the other hand, India—a nation that often confounds experts with its inconsistency in realising its vast potential—demonstrated remarkable resilience and resourcefulness in the face of adversity.

India's response was notably effective. It not only developed indigenous vaccines successfully, but also orchestrated one of the world's largest and fastest vaccination drives, reaching a vast segment of its population in record time. Beyond vaccination efforts, India established an advanced digital infrastructure to manage COVID-19 protocols efficiently. Despite initial scepticism, India navigated the pandemic's challenges with commendable success, fostering a resurgence of national pride through its unexpected achievements.

These observations lead to a reflective inquiry: Does India's adept handling of the COVID-19 crisis signal a one-time occurrence, or does it indicate a broader capability that India potentially has when faced with a crisis?

WITH A deep dive into India's journey since becoming a nation-state in 1947, the first question that crops up in one's mind with the success of its COVID-19 management is whether the success stories in India's history, when considered together, offer broader lessons? And if yes, how can these lessons be replicated during Amrit Kaal for India to become Viksit Bharat@2047?

SINCE INDIA'S Independence in August 1947, India has surpassed expectations when faced with a crisis, be it the foodgrains shortage in the mid-1960s or the open defecation crisis.

India's remarkable resilience captivated me. I delved into its history, searching for a unifying thread—a constant that has enabled the nation to overcome seemingly insurmountable crises.

I found India's unwavering progress, in fact, was achieved through a series of pivotal initiatives launched and implemented by successive governments since 1947. These pivotal initiatives shaped this book and became the central theme. An in-depth analysis of eight pivotal initiatives found that they were largely responsible for the transformational progress in the country's 75-year history.

The key lessons from these initiatives have been distilled with the objective to provide a solid foundation for developing a roadmap for new initiatives during Amrit Kaal.

Extracting broader leadership lessons from these initiatives is valuable. A book filled with narratives of how political leaders, alongside their sherpas, navigated specific crises becomes inherently a study of leadership and problem-solving in action.

Distilled to their essence, the methods, tenacity and resolve employed by these sherpas offer a framework for pivotal initiatives during Amrit Kaal. These principles will undoubtedly be tested in the next 25 years and the path to becoming a developed nation will be arduous and demanding. This will require sustained hard work and a commitment to implementing key pivotal initiatives.

The success stories explored in this book demonstrate their effectiveness across diverse contexts—different historical eras and development stages as well as varying political landscapes and leaders with varied backgrounds and ideologies.

As a result, these stories offer a recipe for success, provided the initiatives are crafted optimally and implemented doggedly.

Igniting Amrit Kaal:
Bold New Initiatives to Propel India's Golden Age
IT IS widely recognised that India's participation in the first three industrial revolutions was limited due to British rule.[1]

After Independence, India pursued import substitution policies to protect domestic industries. While this strategy was to achieve self-reliance, it shielded India from global competition, hindering innovation and efficiency.

India also missed out on some of the early benefits of globalisation in the late 1980s and early 1990s, while several Asian countries made substantial gains by adopting it wholeheartedly.[2]

However, India stands at a pivotal juncture at this moment. The past two decades have witnessed a remarkable transformation, laying a robust foundation for all-round growth during the Amrit Kaal period. A robust digital infrastructure has woven its way across the nation, connecting citizens, businesses and government services. The Aadhaar platform, a unique identification system, has revolutionised access to essential services. The PMJDY has created a never-before-seen financial inclusion of the bottom of the pyramid, fostering economic participation and poverty alleviation.

India stands poised to be a frontrunner in the Fourth Industrial Revolution due to a robust digital foundation. This revolution, marked by the fusion of artificial intelligence (AI) and automation, presents a unique chance for transformation. India's existing digital infrastructure could serve as the bedrock for seamlessly integrating AI solutions. Additionally, Aadhaar could ensure secure data management, vital for AI development. Furthermore, financial inclusion initiatives like the PMJDY could empower the workforce to adapt and flourish in this new technological era.

To take advantage, India must be the first mover in adopting new ideas and technology to be a developed country in the next 25 years. India must adopt a deliberate policy to drive AI innovation, adaptation and proliferation by designing new pivotal initiatives around AI.

FUELLED BY a young population, a growing start-up ecosystem and ongoing economic reforms, India is on track to become the world's third-largest economy by 2027, surpassing Japan and Germany, according to projections.[3]

India's economic growth could likely be accelerated by further refining existing policies. India should remain focused on adding a few more trillions to her GDP.

Nevertheless, this book argues that India's development strategy during Amrit Kaal must prioritise pivotal initiatives that will have a direct impact on citizen well-being and quality of life, rather than solely fixating on GDP growth.[4]

As India journeys towards its centenary of Independence, Amrit Kaal holds immense promise. While economic growth (as reflected in GDP) is crucial, it shouldn't be the sole yardstick of success. Imagine that it's 2047, and that India has become the world's second-largest economy and yet its poorest citizens are malnourished, lack basic education and endure unsanitary conditions. Polluted air hangs heavy and accessing quality healthcare is a constant struggle. This scenario, despite economic might, paints a bleak picture of a nation failing its people.

This skewed development could become a symbol of a failed Amrit Kaal.

SEVERAL PRESSING issues that are intimately linked to 'ease of living' are currently plaguing India—some are already in a critical state, while others teeter on the brink of disaster.

Conceptualisation and implementation of new initiatives would be a significant challenge, because these initiatives would require a near-flawless level of collaboration between the central and state governments. The effectiveness of these initiatives won't solely depend on determined political leadership, but rather on the dedication and competence of the individuals tasked with coordination and implementation—the sherpas.

***

AI-Powered Education Revolution

Transforming India's Classrooms

INDIA'S RECENT ascent to the status of the world's most populous nation, surpassing China in 2023, presents a unique demographic window that could be a potential engine for economic growth in the coming decades.[5]

However, India's K-12 education system is in a crisis that could turn the demographic dividend into a disaster unless a new pivotal initiative is conceptualised and executed early in the Amrit Kaal period.

National data from the past decade has revealed a troubling crisis. Nearly 75 per cent of 10-year-old students lack basic division skills and nearly 30 per cent of 10-to-14-year-olds are reading below their age level.[6]

The second strand of this crisis is the sheer exponential growth in enrolment across all levels in the country. The *Economic Survey 2021–2022* underscores a remarkable surge in school enrolment at all levels from primary to higher secondary.[7]

While surging student enrolment fuels optimism, it also reveals a daunting challenge: scaling up infrastructure and human resources, particularly qualified teachers. With an estimated 200 million students already in K-12 education, the sheer scale of building new schools and training enough teachers presents a seemingly insurmountable hurdle.

Finally, the traditional method of rote memorisation and following strict instructions, the hallmarks of the current system, impedes critical thinking, problem solving and adaptability—skills essential in a rapidly changing AI-driven world.

THE FIRST new pivotal initiative that India should design is to build an AI-empowered education system across the country. AI is currently being implemented with built-in guardrails in several schools in the US. India must not wait for other countries to implement AI-driven school education to avoid potential challenges, but take a lead in a similar way to that of the digital payments system in past 10 years.

The Indian school system could overcome the challenges of K-12 schooling by harnessing AI in various transformative ways, enhancing both teaching methodologies and learning experiences.

AI has been proven to analyse students' learning patterns, strengths and weaknesses and to offer personalised content and learning paths, helping students learn at their own pace and style. It could also provide instant feedback on assignments, freeing up teachers to focus on more complex student needs and personalised instruction methods accordingly. AI could predict students' future learning outcomes based on their learning patterns. This might help in early identification of students who would benefit from additional support, thus ensuring timely intervention in the schooling process.

On the other side of the equation, AI would assist teachers by providing them insights into students' performance and suggesting areas where students might need more attention. It could also help in professional development by identifying skill gaps and recommending training modules.

Just like the eight pivotal initiatives that have shaped India, fostering an AI-powered education system would require a dedicated sherpa. This visionary leader, akin to a Nilekani, should come from the realm of AI and educational technology for driving the initiative forward.

Inspired by Swachh Bharat, this initiative would demand nationwide effort with contributions from everyone. India must focus on building capacity in the existing school system as a priority. In this area, IITs and other engineering graduates in the country could be instrumental in training potential AI leaders across the country's schools. Purposefully designed summer programmes and online modules delivered by these graduates would equip existing teachers across the country with the skills to leverage AI. It would help create AI leaders in all schools across the country in a relatively short time.

Businesses, particularly data providers, could contribute significantly by offering free access to AI platforms for school projects. This would eliminate financial barriers and democratise access to these powerful tools.

Several state governments currently distribute laptops and tablets to students. This programme could be linked to AI-enabled classroom teaching.

With education being a state subject, a collaborative funding model encouraged by Swachh Bharat (potentially a 60-40 Central-State split) could be established. This would ensure a unified approach while empowering states to tailor implementation to their needs.

For example, a partnership between the Indian Government and Khan Academy, a not-for-profit organisation set up by Sal

Khan in the US, could be an essential step towards implementing AI-powered teaching methods in a short time. Khan Academy offers free, online learning resource and educational content for students. Khan Academy has been practising AI-powered adaptive learning in various US-based schools with tailored curriculum to each student's pace and understanding. This could be a boon for India's vast and diverse student population. Khan Academy's existing content can be readily adapted to the Indian curriculum, making it a quicker solution compared to developing entirely new resources.

This initiative holds immense potential for transforming India's education system and make it future-ready. By fostering collaboration between government, industry and academic institutions, India could empower future generations with the tools and knowledge to lead it into an AI-driven world.

***

Defuse the Stunting Time Bomb
Securing India's Future—One Child at a Time

MILLIONS OF INDIA'S preschool children face stunting, a condition with lifelong consequences impacting health, education and future earning potential.[8] This crisis threatens to undermine the nation's demographic dividend, turning a potential advantage into a burden.

To confront this crisis, a groundbreaking, multi-pronged initiative is urgently needed. This isn't just about food security; it requires a holistic approach that transcends departmental boundaries. Collaboration between the Ministries of Health & Family Welfare, Women & Child Development, Agriculture and Rural Development would be crucial for the success of this initiative.

To replicate earlier successful initiatives, this too would need a visionary leader—a sherpa—capable of navigating the complexities of inter-ministerial collaboration. The sherpa would break down departmental silos and spearhead a holistic approach to the problem.

Leadership would be crucial for spearheading a vital campaign centred on the 'First 1,000 Days'—a scientifically proven window critical for a child's healthy development. Drawing inspiration from successful initiatives such as the Swachh Bharat Abhiyan, this campaign should leverage media, social workers and citizen engagement. The Prime Minister's—in a similar way as his involvement in earlier initiatives—should inspire and encourage well-off families to 'adopt' their domestic help during her early months of pregnancy and ensure a glass of milk to her in the morning when she shows up for household work.

The sherpa could help channelise mass media and social media platforms to promote healthy practices such as exclusive breastfeeding if possible or use of milk formula. The campaign would highlight the unparalleled benefits of breast milk for optimal nutrition and immunity, crucial for preventing stunting.

Local governmental units could significantly improve access to critical support for mothers by empowering existing Anganwadis, India's widespread network of rural childcare centres. Anganwadi workers are trusted figures within the community and would be able to effectively mobilise new mothers and address their participation concerns effectively.

Anganwadi centres could be transformed into hubs for connecting mothers with healthcare professionals, nutritionists and lactation consultants remotely via the internet.

Aadhaar and Jan Dhan accounts would be used for exploring options for financial assistance programmes. Direct financial aid helps families cover additional expenses such as prenatal vitamins, nutritious food or childcare, fostering a healthy environment for mothers and children. This combined approach, utilising Aadhaar, the PMJDY and collaboration with NGOs, offers a promising avenue to ensure financial security for families during critical stages of pregnancy and early childhood. By addressing the financial burden, this initiative can significantly contribute to improved maternal and child health outcomes in India.

The Integrated Child Development Services (ICDS) programme has played a vital role in supporting children's wellbeing since 1975. However, to effectively address the current crisis, the programme could benefit from enhancements. A lesson must be learnt from Bangladesh's success, where considerable funds were utilised to prioritise programmes that invest in early childhood development, focusing on interventions from conception to the first 1,000 days of a child's life.

All governmental agencies and ministers would be encouraged to adopt data-driven decision making by tracking children's growth data and adjusting the contours of the initiative accordingly, as was done with the PMJDY when the team realised that several new accounts have zero balance. It would help identify areas requiring focused interventions.

This initiative is not just about social good; it's a strategic investment in India's tomorrow.

India's future rests on the shoulders of its children. A healthy next generation is not just a dream but an economic and social imperative. This new initiative, by leveraging Aadhaar and the PMJDY and by empowering Anganwadis, has the power to avert this crisis and unlock India's true potential.

***

India's Urban Renaissance
From Gridlock to Green Cities

INDIA'S CITIES—FROM bustling metropolises such as Bengaluru to smaller Tier 1, 2, and 3 towns—are in a crisis facing a multitude of challenges. The strain is evident across the spectrum, and the very idea of 'tiers' may soon seem inadequate to capture the complex and interconnected issues plaguing urban India.[9]

Take Bengaluru, India's famed 'Silicon Valley.' This once-thriving tech hub is now a city on edge. In 2022, devastating floods crippled the city, highlighting its crumbling infrastructure. Just two years later, in 2024, Bengaluru faced the opposite extreme—a drought-like situation, that exposed the precarious state of its water resources. These starkly contrasting events, within a short timeframe, showcase the vulnerability of India's urban centres.[10]

Clearly, India's haphazard 'development' of cities would face an urban meltdown if a new pivotal initiative, with acutely needed policy reform supported by modern urban planning and design reforms, isn't implemented in the early stages of Amrit Kaal.

I would argue that it is more important than India getting its export policy right!

The planning process for Indian cities is often dominated by bureaucratic agencies within State Governments, raising concerns about acute lack of citizen participation. In 1992, changes to India's Constitution (73rd and 74th amendments) gave more power to local governments in cities and towns. These amendments aimed to make them more self-governing.[11]

Despite reforms, state governments retain a dominant role in urban planning, mirroring the historical British model where control existed without corresponding accountability.

The second dimension of the crisis stems from the financial strangulation of Indian cities. With only 40 per cent of their revenue generated internally, cities are heavily reliant on funding from the Central and State Governments. This dependence hinders their ability to address critical infrastructure needs and deliver essential services to citizens.[12]

India's urban transformation hinges on a well-designed, comprehensive initiative led by a visionary leader with proven experience in town planning and strong communication skills.

Leading this comprehensive initiative would require collaboration across all states and cities. Developing effective strategies for financial empowerment is crucial. These strategies should focus on increasing local revenue generation through appropriate taxes and user fees, coupled with greater budgetary autonomy for cities. Additionally, decentralisation, and granting more power to local municipalities is essential to ensure optimal responsiveness to citizens' needs and timely interventions.

Similar to the success of Swachh Bharat Mission (the Clean India Mission) in fostering public engagement, citizen participation can be actively encouraged in the urban planning process. This would involve online forums, public hearings and participatory budgeting initiatives. Additionally, implementing a performance-based system that rewards cities for demonstrating effective governance, efficient service delivery and adherence to sustainability principles would create a strong incentive for innovation and high-quality urban development. Technological innovation could offer powerful tools.

The PM Gati Shakti platform could serve as a powerful coordination tool, streamlining infrastructure development and ensuring seamless connectivity across various urban projects.

This multi-faceted new pivotal initiative would hold the key to unlocking the full potential of Indian cities and fostering their transformation into vibrant and thriving economic hubs. It would prioritise financial empowerment through local revenue generation and budgetary control for cities, improved governance with strong citizen participation, sustainable development practices that address environmental concerns and the integration of technological innovation for efficient service delivery.

India must envision a future of thriving green cities, fostering a healthy and sustainable tomorrow for its citizens, by 2047.

***

Bridge the Gap
Unlocking Healthcare Equity

INDIA'S PRIVATE health care sector shines on the global stage, attracting medical tourists with its advanced capabilities and affordability compared to developed nations. However, this success story masks a deep crisis within the country's healthcare system.

Even after more than seventy-five years of Independence, a significant portion of the population struggles to afford basic medical services.[13]

To ensure a truly excellent quality of life for all Indians during the Amrit Kaal period, India must urgently tackle the challenge of healthcare accessibility. A comprehensive, multi-pronged new pivotal initiative must be designed and implemented to bridge the gap and guarantee equitable access to high-quality healthcare services for every citizen within the next twenty-five years.

The core issue isn't necessarily the amount of money being spent (as a percentage of GDP) on healthcare, but rather the absence of a clear vision and well-defined plan and execution. Successive governments have focused on insurance schemes for low-income citizens. However, it is at best being seen as a poor substitute for a strong public healthcare network that alone can be a lasting solution.

Since Independence in 1947, India's healthcare landscape has witnessed a dramatic shift. While the private sector provided only 5-10 per cent of patient care back then, it has grown exponentially. Today, it handles a staggering 82 per cent of outpatient visits, 58 per cent of inpatient expenditure, and a significant 40 per cent of institutional births. This highlights a substantial decline in the public sector's role in healthcare delivery.[14]

India urgently needs to comprehensively reform its healthcare network with robust public healthcare networks as a cornerstone. To modernise India's critically under-resourced public health system, the country urgently needs to leverage technical and financial assistance from organisations such as WHO, UNICEF, and the World Bank, alongside domestic investment.

While the division of health care responsibilities between the Central and State Governments present challenges, it cannot be an excuse for the current shortcomings. India should actively seek best practices from other nations with similar governance structures. Argentina's successful programme SUMAR, implemented in a federal system not unlike India's, offers valuable lessons. By analysing their approach and adapting it to the Indian context, significant improvements can be made in healthcare accessibility and quality.

The pivotal initiative should take a leaf out of the Swachh Bharat Mission book for sharing funding, monitoring and operational efficiency of the healthcare system across the country with all states and districts.

Like all successful initiatives, this pivotal initiative would require a dedicated leader with extensive experience in healthcare in a similar way that Nilekani had deep experience in building the digital backbone of Aadhaar. The sherpa would be required to be supported by a team of public health professionals and potentially the World Bank health expert who helped implement the Argentinian programme.

India possesses a distinct advantage over Argentina in its robust digital infrastructure, particularly because of the Aadhaar system and its associated platforms. This initiative presents a golden opportunity to leverage this advantage by laying the groundwork for a national health delivery platform. This platform, built upon a unified information system, can revolutionise healthcare coordination across the country.

A GST-style council body would be required for making recommendations on issues related to the implementation of a country-wide healthcare programme.

Universal healthcare is not just an incentive, but a fundamental right for every Indian citizen. By 2047, India must strive to ensure accessible and quality healthcare for all, paving the way for a healthier and more productive nation.

***

A Time to Heal

A New Initiative for Environmental Recovery

INDIA CONFRONTS a tangled web of environmental challenges, some longstanding and others emerging from the relentless grip of climate change. Without a pivotal, fast-tracked initiative to tackle these issues head on, the current situation can have dire consequences. Increased urbanisation, population growth and relentless development could act as accelerants to these challenges, threatening to push environmental problems to a breaking point.

The 2021 World Air Quality Report reveals a suffocating reality: a staggering sixty-three of the world's hundred most polluted cities are in India. Topping this dismal list is New Delhi, the nation's capital, holding the unwelcome title of having the world's worst air quality.[15]

Next to air, water pollution is the most pressing environmental issue. India's waterways are choked by a toxic tide. Rampant illegal dumping of raw sewage, silt and garbage has severely contaminated rivers and lakes. This environmental crisis stems from a near total lack of proper sewage infrastructure and an inadequate waste management system.

India, a land blessed with monsoon rains and a vast network of rivers, finds itself grappling with a drinking water crisis. The culprit? An overreliance on an irrigation-centric national water policy, of which 85 per cent of the water is channelled towards agriculture, leaving limited water for drinking, sanitation and industrial use.[16]

Delhi's Ghazipur landfill, a mountain of garbage rivalling the Taj Mahal's height, serves as a stark symbol of India's burgeoning waste management crisis. Every city and town across the nation harbours its own Ghazipur. Waste management has become a pressing environmental issue demanding immediate national attention.

Achieving carbon neutrality by 2060 is only a single thread in the tapestry of environmental challenges that India faces. Unless India addresses the interconnected web of these crises, the impact of carbon neutrality would be insufficient.

THE COMING ten years are undeniably critical for India's environmental future. They provide a pivotal window for India to address its environmental challenges. Failure to act decisively would lead the country past a tipping point, potentially rendering environmental recovery an insurmountable task.

Effectively tackling India's environmental crisis hinges on a pivotal initiative that transcends the current 'siloed' approach by creating a 'super-ministry.' Presently, the Indian Government manages interconnected environmental issues through separate ministries. For example, drinking water falls under one ministry, while river cleaning and management fall under another. This fragmented system creates inefficiencies and hinders progress.

Drawing inspiration from successful and effective pivotal initiatives, a leader with superior skills for working across the related issues would be needed to take the initiative to a logical conclusion. The sherpa would require qualities similar to those of M S Swaminathan, who led the Green Revolution successfully.

While technology alone cannot solve India's environmental challenges, the super-ministry must act as a powerful enabler for collaborative innovation. The sherpa and his team could foster partnerships between industry, local municipal authorities and academic institutions—both Indian and international—for designing India-specific solutions for these issues.

By facilitating knowledge exchange and better resource allocation, the super-ministry would accelerate the adoption and implementation of promising new environmental technologies and practices currently being developed and used across the globe. For example, the 'cap and trading' model currently used in Gujarat to curb particulate air pollution must be made mandatory across the country.[17]

India's Central Pollution Control Board (CPCB) requires a significant revamp to effectively address the nation's intensifying environmental challenges. Strengthening the CPCB's capabilities, air and water quality monitoring infrastructuree, and data analysis expertise, are crucial steps. A more robust CPCB can play a pivotal role in enforcing environmental regulations and ensuring cleaner air and water for all Indians.

Education and public awareness would be an essential part of the initiative and would benefit from the Prime Minister's involvement like in the Swachh Bharat Mission initiative.

WHILE THE success of Amrit Kaal hinges on multiple solutions and targeted efforts, these essential new pivotal initiatives are the foundation stones India must lay ahead of any new policy targeting GDP growth.

***

Acknowledgements

FROM THE collaborative spirit of the boardroom of an energy company to the quiet companionship of my writing desk, this book reflects the invaluable contributions of those around me.

First and foremost, I extend my heartfelt gratitude to Vitasta Publishing for believing in a first-time author and bringing to life my vision of chronicling India's remarkable journey of progress over the past seventy-five years.

I am deeply indebted to Professor Babones, a steadfast champion of the potential of Indian democracy. His unwavering belief not only inspired this work, but also enriched it immeasurably through his generous contribution of the Foreword.

My sincere thanks go to our friend Sherin Qadir, whose artistic talent breathed life into the book's cover, creating a visual representation of its essence.

This endeavour would not have been possible without the unwavering support of my family:

Ray, my eldest son and 'first editor', whose early insights and enthusiastic encouragement were instrumental in shaping the narrative.

Neil, my younger son, whose dedication as a researcher unearthed hidden gems that became invaluable references, adding depth and authenticity to the work.

Preeti, my wife and pillar of strength, who truly lived this book alongside me. Her patience, understanding and support created the space for this dream to take flight.

And to our cat Billy, whose soothing purrs provided much-needed moments of stress relief throughout this journey.

To all who have been part of this journey, directly or indirectly, I offer my deepest gratitude. Your contributions have made this book not just a personal achievement, but a collective celebration of India's enduring spirit.

***

Notes

Foreword

1. https://www.brookings.edu/articles/india-eliminates-extreme-poverty/
2. https://margcompusoft.com/m/indian-bureaucracy/

Introduction

1   https://www.youtube.com/watch?v=V6n9VNbtjeI
2   https://economictimes.indiatimes.com/news/economy/policy/farm-labour-bills-are-steps-in-right-direction-gita-gopinath-chief-economist-imf/articleshow/78687697.cms?from=mdr
3   https://foreignpolicy.com/2021/03/30/modi-india-farmers-protests-agriculture-reforms-rich-versus-poor/
4   https://indianexpress.com/article/opinion/columns/farm-laws-2020-famers-protest-msp-apmc-mandi-system-7125406/
5   https://policyoptions.irpp.org/magazines/obama-at-midterm/the-surprising-failure-of-the-obama-presidency/
6   https://penntoday.upenn.edu/news/capitol-attack -where-does-american-democracy-go-here

7   https://www.brookings.edu/articles/democracy-first-how-the-us-can-prevail-in-the-political-systems-competition-with-the-ccp/

8   https://www.aspistrategist.org.au/are-indian-democracys-weaknesses-inherent/

9   https://www.livemint.com/economy/the-history-behind-hindu-rate-of-growth-in-charts-11678370005198.html

10   https://www.globaltimes.cn/page/202209/1274920.shtml

11   https://foreignpolicy.com/2022/10/04/china-india-economic-gap-tooze/

12   https://www.economist.com/weeklyedition/2022-05-14

13   https://amritt.com/the-india-expert-blog/economics-nobel-laureate-spence-india-is-the-outstanding-performer/

14   https://www.indiatoday.in/india-today-conclave/2023

15   https://www.business-standard.com/podcast/current-affairs/what-will-it-take-to-make-india-a-developed-nation-in-the-next-25-years-122081600058_1.html

16   https://www.thecaravelgu.com/blog/2023/3/5/analysis-can-india-become-a-developed-country-in-25-years

17   https://www.businesstoday.in/magazine/economy/story/corporate-indias-vision-for-india-for-the-next-25-years-344033-2022-08-08

18   https://www.jfklibrary.org/visit-museum/exhibits/past-exhibits/moon-shot-jfk-and-space-exploration

19   https://medium.com/wordsthatmatter/never-waste-a-serious-w%C4%93ij%C4%AB-%E5%8D%B1%E6%9C%BA-34d40c6768d2

20   https://carnegieendowment.org/2019/01/16/is-democracy-problem-pub-78137

21   https://www.rpc.senate.gov/policy-papers/a-decade-of-repairing-damage-done-by-obamacare#:~:text=Ten%20years%20after%20Obamacare%20w

22 https://economictimes.indiatimes.com/news/politics-and-nation/modi-govt-killing-off-mgnrega-by-cutting-budgets-delaying-payments-alleges-congress/articleshow/99790020.cms

23 www.thehindu.com/business/budget/budget-2023-mgnrega-budget-slashed-33-from-this-years-revised-estimates/article66458555.ece

24 https://www.brookings.edu/articles/six-ways-trump-has-sabotaged-the-affordable-care-act/

25 http://www.gajendrahaldea.in/pdf/Flier-for-book-Indian-Highways.pdf

26 https://www.indiatoday.in/india/story/aadhaar-journey-kargil-supreme-court-1349503-2018-09-

27 https://www.business-standard.com/india-news/jan-dhan-helps-centre-tackling-corruption-in-direct-benefits-transfers-123082700732_1.html

28 https://www.business-standard.com/about/what-is-ondc

Union of Princely States with India

1 https://www.nationalarchives.gov.uk/education/resources/indian-independence/us-reaction-uk-withdrawal/

2 https://www.bbc.com/news/world-asia-india-66594520

3 https://www.abc.net.au/news/2022-08-15/india-marks-75-years-of-independence-people-share-hopes-future/101312202

4 https://www.thequint.com/news/world/franklin-roosevelt-role-in-india-independence-british-rule-churchill

5 https://theprint.in/pageturner/excerpt/britain-had-become-paranoid-of-india-us-friendship-nehrus-letter-to-roosevelt-didnt-help/586581/

6 https://www.iwm.org.uk/history/how-winston-churchill-and-the-conservative-party-lost-the-1945-election

7   Walter Reid, *Keeping the Jewel in the Crown: The British Betrayal of India*, Birlinn, 2016

8   https://academic.oup.com/book/27565/chapter-abstract/197586 969?redirectedFrom=fulltext

9   https://academic.oup.com/book/3076/chapter-abstract/1438599 74?redirectedFrom=fulltext

10   https://frontline.thehindu.com/other/article30182839.ece

11   https://api.parliament.uk/historic-hansard/commons/1947/ jun/03/india-transfer-of-power

12   https://www.outlookindia.com/website/story/the-british-pm- who-oversaw-indias-independence/295156

13   https://www.thebetterindia.com/198487/v-p-menon-sardar- patel-history-jammu-kashmir-accession-india-unification/

14   https://www.britishempire.co.uk/maproom/india/vpmenon.htm

15   https://www.hindustantimes.com/india-news/mountbattens-last- plan-for-independence-all-you-need-to-know-about-the-june-3- 1947-plan-101622694800571.html

16   https://academic.oup.com/book/27565/chapter-abstract/197586 969?redirectedFrom=fulltext

17   Ian Copland (1993), "Lord Mountbatten and the Integration of the Indian States: A Reappraisal", The Journal of Imperial and Commonwealth History, 21(2): 385–408, doi:10.1080/03086539308582896

18   http://mainstreamweekly.net/article10600.html

19   https://www.tribuneindia.com/news/archive/comment/ remembering-mountbatten-s-june-3-plan-599572

20   https://indianexpress.com/article/explained/remembering-vp- menons-role-in-accession-of-jk-and-other-states-6039385/

21   https://www.inc.in/brief-history-of-congress/1945-1955

22   https://pib.gov.in/FeaturesDeatils. aspx?NoteId=150588&ModuleId=2

23 https://www.india.gov.in/spotlight/ek-bharat-shreshtha-bharat#:~:text=The%20Ek%20Bharat%20Shrestha%20Bharat,greater%20mutual%20understanding%20amongst%20them.

24 https://economictimes.indiatimes.com/industry/services/education/reasons-why-the-neps-move-to-teaching-in-mother-tongue-could-transform-learning-in-india/articleshow/89691532.cms?from=mdr

Rebuilding India without a 'Marshall Plan'

1   https://www.rediff.com/money/2003/jan/18iit2.htm

2   https://academic.oup.com/book/27565/chapter-abstract/197586969?redirectedFrom=fulltext

3   https://www.archives.gov/milestone-documents/marshall-plan#:~:text=On%20December%2019%2C%201947%2C%20President,known%20as%20the%20Marshall%20Plan.

4   https://www.linkedin.com/pulse/reviving-manufacturing-india-iii-rise-fall-engineering-prabir-jana/

5   https://indianexpress.com/article/india/british-reduced-india-to-one-of-the-poorest-countries-shashi-tharoor-4439070/

6   https://www.asianstudies.org/publications/eaa/archives/the-history-of-economic-development-in-india-since-independence/

7   https://royalsocietypublishing.org/doi/10.1098/rsnr.1946.0013

8   https://www.linkedin.com/pulse/hill-av-1944-report-government-india-scientific-research-das/

9   https://pdfs.semanticscholar.org/a13d/b634e1a4bd9f1e52ec88c3019b195e1c1b14.pdf

10 https://www.iitb.ac.in/en/about-iit-bombay/institute-history#:~:text=IIT%20Bombay%20was%20established%20with,government%20of%20the%20then%20USSR

11 https://en.wikipedia.org/wiki/List_of_Indian_engineering_colleges_before_Independence#cite_note-report_UEC2-4

12 https://asianlite.com/2021/columns/lite-blogs/the-men-who-created-an-enduring-nursery-of-excellence/

13 https://www.iitsystem.ac.in/history

14 https://www.aicte-india.org/education/institutions/IITs#:~:text=The%20IITs%20were%20created%20to,India%20after%20independence%20in%201947

15 https://www.heritagetimes.in/nalini-ranjan-sarkar-the-real-father-of-iit/

16 https://scroll.in/article/801621/how-the-iits-were-born-and-their-philosophies-determined

17 https://ummid.com/news/2021/december/05.12.2021/iit-the-men-who-created-an-enduring-nursery-of-excellence.html

18 https://www.ndtv.com/book-excerpts/book-excerpt-nehrus-role-in-carving-special-status-for-iit-2156293#:~:text=%22Here%20in%20the%20place%20of,and%20this%20world%20today...

19 https://www.iitb.ac.in/en/about-iit-bombay

20 https://en.wikipedia.org/wiki/History_of_Indian_Institutes_of_Technology

21 https://philoneistblog.wordpress.com/2020/05/25/the-heritage-of-the-iits/

22 https://presidentofindia.nic.in/index.php/speeches/address-honble-president-india-smt-droupadi-murmu-closing-ceremony-diamond-jubilee

23 https://www.thehindubusinessline.com/news/education/iits-have-built-brand-india-globally-says-pm-modi/article24664560.ece

24 https://www.business-standard.com/india-news/iit-madras-establishes-first-international-campus-in-tanzania-s-zanzibar-123110600630_1.html

25 https://www.hindustantimes.com/cities/delhi-news/
    mtech-at-iit-delhi-s-abu-dhabi-campus-to-start-in-
    february-101704906885346.html

26 https://economictimes.indiatimes.com/news/india/iit-kharagpur-
    to-set-up-institute-in-malaysia/articleshow/96490485.
    cms?from=mdr

From 'Begging Bowl' to 'Breadbasket'

1   https://theprint.in/past-forward/hungry-india-a-nawabi-
    us-president-mexican-blood-the-real-story-of-green-
    revolution/835649/

2   https://www.cabidigitallibrary.org/doi
    pf/10.5555/20220000345#:~:text=Independent%20India%20
    was%20born%20hungry,people%20dead%20(Maharatna%20
    1996).

3   https://www.redcross.org.uk/stories/our-movement/our-history/
    india-partition-the-red-cross-response-to-the-refugee-crisis

4   https://www.niti.gov.in/sites/default/files/2023-07/Aggricultrue_
    Amritkal.pdf

5   https://www.asianstudies.org/publications/eaa/archives/the-
    history-of-economic-development-in-india-since-independence/

6   John H. Perkins, *Geopolitics and the Green Revolution: Wheat,
    Genes, and the Cold War,* Oxford University Press, 1997, p. 152

7   https://resource.rockarch.org/story/the-rockefeller-foundations-
    agriculture-program-in-india-1950s-1960s/

8   https://www.thehindubusinessline.com/india-at-75/overcoming-
    food-emergencies-through-imports-from-us-via-pl480/
    article65753881.ece

9   https://academic.oup.com/book/31866/chapter-abstract/267515
    079?redirectedFrom=fulltext

10 https://www.statista.com/statistics/1066922/population-india-historical/

11 https://archive.md/20130126005836/http://www.hindu.com/fline/fl1505/15051130.htm#selection-101.294-101.613

12 https://www.preventionweb.net/news/battling-centurys-worst-drought-indias-farmers-revive-traditional-grains

13 https://www.thehindubusinessline.com/india-at-75/overcoming-food-emergencies-through-imports-from-us-via-pl480/article65753881.ece

14 https://www.thestatesman.com/opinion/green-revolutioni-1502997253.html

15 https://www.indiatoday.in/magazine/guest-column/story/20001127-a-tribute-to-the-spearhead-of-indias-green-revolution-778501-2000-11-26

16 https://www.nytimes.com/1964/07/26/archives/shastri-returns-to-work-as-hunger-stalks-indians-public-unrest-is.html

17 https://www.thehindu.com/news/national/tamil-nadu/the-architects-of-green-revolution-from-tn/article65210677.ece

18 https://indianexpress.com/article/opinion/columns/no-one-asks-the-farmers-genetically-modified-gm-seeds-mustard-canola-oil-3086481/

19 https://academic.oup.com/book/26111/chapter-abstract/194115650?redirectedFrom=fulltext

20 https://www.indiatoday.in/magazine/guest-column/story/20001127-a-tribute-to-the-spearhead-of-indias-green-revolution-778501-2000-11-26

21 https://www.outlookindia.com/national/ms-swaminathan-father-of-india-s-green-revolution-passes-away-at-98-news-321146

22 https://theprint.in/theprint-profile/chidambaram-subramaniam-the-force-behind-indias-green-revolution-who-never-took-credit-for-it/1342059/

23 https://csacademy.in/latest-news/chidambaram-subramaniam-green-leader-died-november-7th/

24 https://www.outlookindia.com/national/ms-swaminathan-father-of-india-s-green-revolution-passes-away-at-98-news-321146#:~:text=In%20a%20country%20that%20extensively,struggling%20with%20lack%20of%20food

25 https://www.nytimes.com/2000/11/10/world/chidambaram-subramaniam-india-s-green-rebel-90-dies.html

26 https://academic.oup.com/book/3199/chapter-abstract/144125512?redirectedFrom=fulltext

27 https://www.thestatesman.com/opinion/green-revolutioni-1502997253.html

28 https://www.earth-policy.org/books/bng/bngch6

29 https://content.time.com/time/subscriber/article/0,33009,842326,00.html

30 https://www.thestatesman.com/opinion/green-revolutioni-1502997253.html

31 https://www.theguardian.com/global-development-professionals-network/2015/apr/30/how-to-end-hunger-lessons-from-the-father-of-indias-green-revolution

32 https://www.outlookindia.com/national/ms-swaminathan-father-of-india-s-green-revolution-passes-away-at-98-news-321146#:~:text=In%20a%20country%20that%20extensively,struggling%20with%20lack%20of%20food

33 https://www.thehindu.com/news/cities/chennai/ms-swaminathan-transformed-the-country-from-a-begging-bowl-to-a-breadbasket/article67418134.ece

34 https://scroll.in/article/670110/a-tv-channel-for-farmers-could-be-useful-but-past-experience-suggests-otherwise

35 https://www.business-standard.com/india-news/m-s-

swaminathan-scientist-who-made-india-self-sufficient-in-food-dies-123092800625_1.html

'Smiling Buddha' to 'Operation Shakti'

1   https://www.armscontrol.org/act/1998-05/news-briefs/india-conducts-nuclear-tests-pakistan-follows-suit#:~:text=Indian%20Prime%20Minister%20Atal%20Bihari,to%20have%20sub%2Dkiloton%20yields

2   https://www.icanw.org/nuclear_weapons_history

3   https://diplomacybeyond.com/indias-role-in-the-non-aligned-movement/

4   https://www.un.org/en/chronicle/article/united-nations-and-disarmament-treaties#:~:text=After%20an%20egregiously%20irresponsible%2015,Commission%20on%2029%20July%201954.

5   https://www.thehindu.com/news/national/not-signing-the-npt-one-of-indias-most-consequential-decisions-former-envoy/article65635838.ecehttps://www.nonproliferation.org/wp-content/uploads/npr/paul61.pdf

6   https://history.state.gov/milestones/1961-1968/npt

7   https://disarmament.unoda.org/wmd/nuclear/npt/#:~:text=Opened%20for%20signature%20in%201968,the%20five%20nuclear%2Dweapon%20States 3 DOCUMENTS ON AUSTRALIAN FOREIGN POLICY, Australia and the Nuclear Non-Proliferation Treaty 1945–1974 WAYNE REYNOLDS and DAVID LEE

8   https://www.world-nuclear.org/information-library/safety-and-security/non-proliferation/india,-china-npt.aspx

9   https://library.fes.de/pdf-files/iez/global/05793.pdf

10 https://www.thedailystar.net/news/us-fleet-in-bay-of-bengal-a-game-of-deception

11 https://www.armscontrol.org/act/2008-06/looking-back-1998-indian-pakistani-nuclear-tests

12 https://indianexpress.com/article/explained/explained-history/operation-smiling-buddha-nuclear-first-test-pokhran-history-8616714/

13 https://history.state.gov/milestones/1961-1968/npt

14 https://carnegieendowment.org/2022/07/18/india-pub-87397

15 https://www.indiatoday.in/magazine/cover-story/story/19870331-dr-aq-khans-pak-n-bomb-revelation-brings-prospect-of-nuke-arms-race-to-the-subcontinent-798697-1987-03-30

16 https://www.nonproliferation.org/wp-content/uploads/npr/paul61.pdf

17 https://disarmament.unoda.org/wmd/nuclear/ctbt/#:~:text=On%2010%20September%2C%20the%20General,at%20the%20earliest%20possible%20date.

18 https://muse.jhu.edu/article/487181/summary

19 Rajiv Gandhi, "A World Free of Nuclear Weapons," Proposal Presented at the U.N. General assembly, Third Special Session on Disarmament, New York, June 9, 1988, reprinted in India and Disarmament, pp. 280–94.

20 https://theprint.in/past-forward/how-pokhran-nuclear-tests-kicked-off-a-year-that-changed-india-pakistan-ties-forever/254235/

21 https://www.eurasiareview.com/10052023-how-india-was-forced-to-conduct-the-nuclear-tests-of-1998-analysis/

22 https://www.armscontrol.org/act/2008-06/looking-back-1998-indian-pakistani-nuclear-tests

23 https://www.orfonline.org/expert-speak/how-india-was-forced-to-conduct-the-nuclear-tests-of-1998

24 https://timesofindia.indiatimes.com/india/remembering-

indias-missile-man-apj-abdul-kalam-his-10-big-achievements/
articleshow/94865613.cms

25 https://www.indiatoday.in/magazine/articles-on-apj-abdul-
kalam-from-india-today/story/19940415-after-string-of-recent-
successes-india-missile-programme-gains-in-maturity-and-
stature-809044-1999-11-29

26 https://www.nytimes.com/2015/07/28/world/asia/apj-abdul-
kalam-ex-president-who-pushed-a-nuclear-india-dies-at-83.html

27 https://www.nbcnews.com/id/wbna3340755

28 https://www.vifindia.org/sites/default/files/national-security-vol-
1-issue-1-document-statement-to-parliament.pdf

29 https://www.orfonline.org/expert-speak/the-1998-pokhran-
nuclear-tests

30 https://www.orfonline.org/research/re-examining-india-s-
nuclear-doctrine#:~:text=The%20Indian%20Government%20
announced%20its,'No%20First%20Use'%20policy.

31 https://timesofindia.indiatimes.com/india/no-first-use-nuclear-
policy-explained/articleshow/70844818.cms

32 https://www.orfonline.org/expert-speak/the-1998-pokhran-
nuclear-tests/

33 https://timesofindia.indiatimes.com/blogs/ashoks-statecraft/
jaswant-talbatt-talk-and-india-us-strategic-engagement-a-legacy-
of-jaswant-singh-the-foreign-minister-at-the-crucial-juncture-of-
indias-international-engagement/

34 https://www.hindustantimes.com/india/my-dinner-with-jaswant/
story-Wog8GQbxKBDBfsaomtfSwJ.html

35 https://www.nytimes.com/1998/05/12/world/india-sets-3-
nuclear-blasts-defying-a-worldwide-ban-tests-bring-a-sharp-
outcry.html.

36 https://www.vifindia.org/2018/may/24/20-years-of-india-s-
nuclearisation-retrospect-and-prospect

37 https://issi.org.pk/wp-content/uploads/2016/07/SS_
No_4_2015_Dr-Rashid-Ahmed.pdf

38 https://www.cfr.org/backgrounder/us-india-nuclear-deal

39 https://www.brookings.edu/wp-content/
uploads/2017/07/2ndmodi_o_einhornwps.pdf

40 https://www.newindianexpress.com/nation/2018/Jan/19/india-
becomes-member-of-australia-group-1758807.html

41 https://carnegieendowment.org/2016/06/30/india-s-nuclear-
doctrine-debate-pub-63950

42 https://fas.org/publication/indias-nuclear-arsenal-takes-a-big-
step-forward/

44 https://www.nytimes.com/1998/05/16/world/nuclear-anxiety-
india-new-delhi-premier-indicates-resolve-produce-nuclear.html

India's 'New Deal' Infrastructure Development through Public–Private Partnership

1. https://www.globaltimes.cn/page/202401/1304656.shtml

2 https://academic.oup.com/book/7527/chapter-abstract/1524703
99?redirectedFrom=fulltext

3 https://www.spglobal.com/en/research-insights/articles/
the-missing-piece-in-indias-economic-growth-story-robust-
infrastructure

4 https://www.brookings.edu/articles/infrastructure-in-india-the-
economics-of-transition-from-public-to-private-provision/

5 https://www.sciencedirect.com/science/article/pii/
S0263786316301090

6 https://www3.weforum.org/docs/Migration_Impact_Cities_
report_2017_low.pdf

7 https://www.sciencedirect.com/science/article/abs/pii/
S0301421503002830

8   https://www.business-standard.com/article/economy-policy/grid-collapse-third-failure-in-two-years-102080101056_1.html

9   https://assets.publishing.service.gov.uk/media/57a089f5ed915d3c fd0004ee/61270-Electricity-insecurity-impact-SMEs-010914.pdf

10   https://www.researchgate.net/publication/276198990_Impacts_ of_Electricity_Access_to_Rural_SMEs

11   https://www.adb.org/sites/default/files/publication/157241/adbi-rp59.pdf

12   https://www.rba.gov.au/publications/bulletin/2014/jun/pdf/bu-0614-4.pdf

13   https://www.spglobal.com/en/research-insights/articles/ the-missing-piece-in-indias-economic-growth-story-robust-infrastructure

14   https://blogs.worldbank.org/en/digital-development/how-does-infrastructure-support-sustainable-growth

15   https://www.epw.in/journal/1997/16/policy-watch-specials/all-dressed-and-nowhere-go-india-infrastructure-report.html

16   https://www.ndtvprofit.com/opinion/infravisioning-what-next-for-ppp-after-a-quarter-of-a-century

17   https://www.worldbank.org/content/dam/Worldbank/document/ Development%20Research%20Group/Highway%20to%20 Success%20The%20Impact%20of%20the%20Golden%20 Quadrilateral.pdf

18   https://archive.md/20120731160327/http://www. financialexpress.com/news/contractors-take-the-sheen-off-golden-quadrilateral/826471/0

19   https://cag.gov.in/uploads/media/ppp-project-05de4f5a51b7 fa2-72318731-20201016153105.pdf

20   https://www.moneylife.in/article/why-indians-need-to-understand-the-importance-of-gajendra-haldeas-contribution-to-the-nation/64932.html

21 https://www.mckinsey.com/~/media/mckinsey/dotcom/client_
service/infrastructure/pdfs/01%20building%20india.ashx

22 https://www.financialexpress.com/opinion/gajendra-haldea-
father-of-indias-infra-ppp/2172714/

23 https://www.imf.org/external/np/seminars/eng/2010/spr/lic/
forum/index.htm

24 https://documents1.worldbank.org/curated/
en/855761468041672781/pdf/Private-participation-in-the-
Indian-power-sector-lessons-from-two-decades-of-experience.pdf

25 https://www.power-technology.com/projects/dabhol-combined-
cycle-power-plant-maharashtra-india/?cf-view

26 https://www.youtube.com/watch?v=WMxVPopk-Q8

27 http://gajendrahaldea.in/pdf/Obituaries.pdf

28 http://www.gajendrahaldea.in/pdf/GH-Resume-220814-Clean-
FINAL.pdf

29 http://www.gajendrahaldea.in/download/Handshake_IFC.pdf

30 http://www.gajendrahaldea.in/pdf/Hyderabad-Metro-MSS.pdf

31 https://www.hindustantimes.com/india-news/atal-setu-
inauguration-live-updates-narendra-modi-mumbai-trans-
harbour-link-news-today-12-january-2024-101705036206222.
html

Digital Identity to Billions

1 https://www.newyorker.com/magazine/2011/10/03/the-i-d-man

2 https://publications.azimpremjiuniversity.edu.in/1766/

3 https://anderson-review.ucla.edu/addressing-its-lack-of-an-id-
system-india-registers-1-2-billion-in-a-decade/

4 https://www.oecd.org/gov/innovative-government/India-case-
study-UAE-report-2018.pdf

5 https://www.thestatesman.com/opinion/the-85-paise-
riddle-1502398034.html

6   https://pathwayscommission.bsg.ox.ac.uk/sites/default/
files/2019-09/lessons_from_aadhaar.pdf

7   https://www.sciencedirect.com/science/article/abs/pii/
S1059056012001293

8   https://pathwayscommission.bsg.ox.ac.uk/sites/default/
files/2019-09/lessons_from_aadhaar.pdf

9   https://www.researchgate.net/publication/338211667_Illegal_
Migration_and_Strategic_Challenges_A_Case_Study_of_
Undocumented_Migration_from_Bangladesh_to_India

10 Dixit, J. N. (2 August 2003). Pg 56–60 Dixit, JN, "India-
Pakistan in War & Peace", Routledge, 2002. ISBN
9780203301104. Retrieved 15 June 2012

11 https://www.indiatoday.in/india/story/aadhaar-journey-kargil-
supreme-court-1349503-2018-09-26

12 https://timesofindia.indiatimes.com/business/sc-holds-
aadhaar-valid-a-brief-history-of-a-unique-identity-project/
articleshow/65975093.cms

13 https://www.newyorker.com/magazine/2011/10/03/the-i-d-man

14 https://www.business-standard.com/article/press-releases/nandan-m-
nilekani-appointed-as-chairperson-of-uidai-109062500107_1.html

15 https://www.w3summit.io/srikanth-nadhamuni.php

16 https://www.forbesindia.com/article/big-bet/how-nandan-
nilekani-took-aadhaar-past-the-tipping-point/36259/1

17 https://economictimes.indiatimes.com/news/politics-and-nation/
government-asks-uidai-to-use-biometric-data-gathered-by-the-
home-ministry/articleshow/13910700.cms?from=mdr

18 https://timesofindia.indiatimes.com/india/ranjana-sonawane-is-
now-a-12-digit-no-/articleshow/6654987.cms

19 https://www.albrightstonebridge.com/news/aadhaar-
india%E2%80%99s-identification-system

20 Under "Dashboard Summary," see Aadhaar enrollment as of March 2014 in the chart "Aadhaar Trend" Available at https://portal.uidai.gov.in/uidwebportal/dashboard.do

21 https://direct.mit.edu/itgg/article-pdf/9/1-2/85/705311/inov_a_00204.pdf

22 https://economictimes.indiatimes.com/news/economy/policy/nandan-nilekani-impresses-narendra-modi-arun-jaitley-gets-aadhaar-a-lifeline/articleshow/38940461.cms?from=mdr

23 https://www.thehindu.com/news/national/nilekani-resigns-as-uidai-chairman/article5781144.ece

24 https://thewire.in/government/arun-jaitley-introduces-money-bill-on-aadhar-in-lok-sabha

25 https://uidai.gov.in/images/The_Aadhaar_Enrolment_and_Update_Regulations_2016_with_Schedules.pdf

26 https://egazette.gov.in/WriteReadData/2017/175141.pdf

27 https://indianexpress.com/article/explained/explained-what-are-the-latest-changes-to-aadhaar-5825707/

28 https://egovstandards.gov.in/sites/default/files/2021-07/Guidelines%20on%20Mobile%20as%20Digital%20identity.pdf

29 https://uidai.gov.in/en/about-uidai/unique-identification-authority-of-india.html#:~:text=As%20on%2029th%20September%202023,to%20the%20residents%20of%20India

30 https://www.indiatoday.in/business/story/exclusive-world-sees-india-as-incubator-of-innovation-pm-modi-on-upi-aadhaar-success-2426926-2023-08-26

Financial Inclusion of the Bottom of the Pyramid

1 https://www.hindustantimes.com/india-news/pm-narendra-modi-s-pradhan-mantri-jan-dhan-yojana-crosses-500-million-accounts-empowering-women-and-rural-areas-101692428279687.html

2   https://economictimes.indiatimes.com/nation-world/
     top-six-political-slogans-and-their-impact/garibi-hatao/
     slideshow/23599157.cms

3   https://www.thequint.com/news/india/indira-gandhi-bank-
     nationalisation-1969-morarji-congress#read-more

4   https://knowledge.wharton.upenn.edu/article/financial-inclusion-
     india-aims-move-beyond-bank-accounts/

5   https://ufa.worldbank.org/en/ufa

6   https://www.indiatoday.in/india/story/jan-dhan-yojana-pm-
     modi-nda-government-206033-2014-08-28

7   https://www.mudra.org.in/Default/DownloadFile/Success%20
     Stories.pdf

8   https://www.narendramodi.in/pm-launches-pradhan-mantri-jan-
     dhan-yojana-6503

9   https://www.bbc.com/news/10227680

10   https://theprint.in/opinion/its-2021-and-the-indian-bureaucracy-
     remains-the-greatest-impediment-to-progress/587750/

11   https://eastasiaforum.org/2014/07/03/the-unintended-legacy-of-
     manmohan-singh/

12   https://knowledge.wharton.upenn.edu/article/financial-inclusion-
     india-aims-move-beyond-bank-accounts/

13   https://www.elibrary.imf.org/display/book/9798400223525/
     CH007.xml#:~:text=Financial%20inclusion%20in%20India%20
     was,financial%20institution%20(Figure%207.1)

14   https://knowledge.wharton.upenn.edu/article/financial-inclusion-
     india-aims-move-beyond-bank-accounts/

15   https://knowledge.wharton.upenn.edu/article/financial-inclusion-
     india-aims-move-beyond-bank-accounts/

16   https://publishing.cdlib.org/ucpressebooks/
     view?docId=ft1g500470;query=france;brand=ucpress

17   https://www.jstor.org/stable/43946624

18 https://www.downtoearth.org.in/environment/jan-dhan-yojana-how-the-government-started-15-million-bank-accounts-in-one-day-46077

19 https://economictimes.indiatimes.com/news/economy/policy/pm-jan-dhan-yojana-launched-1-5-crore-bank-accounts-opened-in-a-day/articleshow/41093413

20 https://indianexpress.com/article/explained/explained-economics/how-jan-dhan-has-had-a-transformative-impact-on-financial-banking sector-9538734/

21 https://economictimes.indiatimes.com/industry/banking/finance/banking/banks-open-10-3-cr-jan-dhan-accounts-issue-7-28-cr-rupay-cards/articleshow/45730379.cms?from=mdr

22 https://assets.kpmg.com/content/dam/kpmg/in/pdf/2017/10/PMJDY.pdf

23 https://www.moneycontrol.com/news/business/around-80-of-jan-dhan-accounts-opened-through-business-correspondent-channels-says-uco-bank-official-11289231.html

24 https://pib.gov.in/newsite/printrelease.aspx?relid=126439

25 www.theweek.in/theweek/cover/2023/05/26/union-minister-of-state-for-finance-bhagwat-karad-about-economic-progress-under-modi-government.html

26 https://www.livemint.com/news/india/rupay-card-issuances-fall-far-behind-jan-dhan-bank-accounts-11605271813361.html

27 https://www.business-standard.com/article/finance/sbi-yes-bank-lead-in-zero-balance-accounts-under-jan-dhan-yojana-115012100174_1.html

28 https://www.businesstoday.in/magazine/deep-dive/story/financial-inclusion-challenge-how-have-initiatives-like-jan-dhan-mudra-loans-and-many-more-fared-so-far-410749-2023-12-26

29 https://www.thehindubusinessline.com/economy/direct-benefit-transfer-seen-reducing-zerobalance-accounts-in-pm-scheme/article8573077.ece

30 https://www.thehindubusinessline.com/economy/direct-benefit-transfer-seen-reducing-zerobalance-accounts-in-pm-scheme/article8573077.ece

31 https://www.womensworldbanking.org/insights/report-making-jan-dhan-work-for-rural-women/

32 https://www.deccanherald.com/india/millions-of-people-brought-into-financial-mainstream-modi-on-9-years-of-pm-jan-dhan-yojana-2664004

33 https://www.hindustantimes.com/india-news/pm-narendra-modi-s-pradhan-mantri-jan-dhan-yojana-crosses-500-million-accounts-empowering-women-and-rural-areas-101692428279687.html

34 https://www.womensworldbanking.org/insights/report-making-jan-dhan-work-for-rural-women/

35 https://www.business-standard.com/india-news/jan-dhan-helps-centre-tackling-corruption-in-direct-benefits-transfers-123082700732_1.html

36 https://www.deccanherald.com/india/delhi/jam-trinity-curbed-corruption-rs-275-lakh-crore-prevented-from-going-into-wrong-hands-droupadi-murmu-2872546

Ushering in Behavioural Change among Billions

1 https://www.healthabitat.com/raising-the-toilet-issue-in-india/

2 https://www.thehindu.com/news/national/Swacch-Bharat-Mission/article60350320.ece

3 https://www.indiatoday.in/india/story/narendra-modi-independence-day-speech-full-text-red-fort-204216-2014-08-15

4 https://www.ncbi.nlm.nih.gov/pmc/articles/PMC8552289/

5   https://www.ncbi.nlm.nih.gov/pmc/articles/PMC10798809/

6   https://www.worldbank.org/en/topic/sanitation

7   https://www.worldbank.org/en/news/feature/2011/01/13/india-cost-of-inadequate-sanitation

8   https://www.who.int/southeastasia/news/speeches/detail/the-health-and-economic-cost-of-poor-sanitation

9   https://www.ncbi.nlm.nih.gov/pmc/articles/PMC10282129/#:~:text=It%20has%20been%20estimated%20that,million%20underweight%20children%20%5B3%5D.

10 https://timesofindia.indiatimes.com/india/more-than-40-of-the-worlds-stunted-children-live-in-india-report/articleshow/66251572.cms

11 https://dro.deakin.edu.au/articles/journal_contribution/Effects_of_sanitation_and_hygiene_perceptions_on_international_travelers_health_travel_plans_and_trip_experiences_in_India/24003705

12 https://www.unicef.org/india/topics/water-supply#:~:text=In%202015%2C%20nearly%20half%20of,Country%20Programme%20in%20India%2C%20where

13 https://loksabhadocs.nic.in/Refinput/New_Reference_Notes/English/Manual%20Scavengers%20welfare%20and%20Rehabilitation.pdf

14 https://pib.gov.in/newsite/erelcontent.aspx?relid=44717#:~:text=India%20's%20first%20nationwide%20program,gave%20emphasis%20on%20toilet%20construction.

15 https://www.researchgate.net/publication/277419703_An_untold_story_of_policy_failure_The_Total_Sanitation_Campaign_in_India

16 https://www.centreforpublicimpact.org/case-study/total-sanitation-campaign-india

17 https://bpb-us-w2.wpmucdn.com/web.sas.upenn.edu/dist/1/140/files/2016/06/CHAPTER-17_-Purity-pollution-and-untouchability_-1r06ybb.pdf

18 https://normativenarratives.com/2014/07/17/economic-outlook-malnutrition-and-sanitation-in-india/

19 https://pib.gov.in/newsite/erelcontent.aspx?relid=44717#:~:text=India%20's%20first%20nationwide%20program,gave%20emphasis%20on%20toilet%20construction.

20 https://www.gatesfoundation.org/our-work/programs/global-growth-and-opportunity/water-sanitation-and-hygiene/reinvent-the-toilet-challenge-and-expo

21 https://www.narendramodi.in/c-m-for-successful-implementation-of-total-sanitation-project-3546

22 https://www.business-standard.com/india-news/pm-modi-calls-for-cleanliness-drive-on-oct-1-ahead-of-gandhi-jayanti-123092900215_1.html

23 economictimes.indiatimes.com/news/politics-and-nation/clean-india-mission-beyond-politics-pm-modi/articleshow/44079411.cms?from=mdr

24 https://www.centreforpublicimpact.org/case-study/total-sanitation-campaign-india

25 https://www.youtube.com/watch?v=A91OOQJwRFE

26 https://sdgs.un.org/partnerships/swachh-bharat-abhiyan-clean-india-mission

27 https://www.worldbank.org/en/about/people/p/parameswaran-iyer

28 https://www.worldbank.org/en/about/people/p/parameswaran-iyer

29 https://gh.bmj.com/content/4/5/e001892

30 https://infinitylearn.com/surge/english/article/swachh-bharat-abhiyan-brand-ambassadors/

31 https://sdgs.un.org/partnerships/swachh-bharat-abhiyan-clean-india-mission

32 https://pib.gov.in/PressReleasePage.aspx?PRID=1759593

33 https://swachhindia.ndtv.com/parliament-panel-recommends-law-penalise-spitting-throwing-garbage-public-places-31020/

34 https://economictimes.indiatimes.com/news/india/pm-modi-launches-second-phases-of-swachh-bharat-mission-urban-amrut/articleshow/86674692.cms?from=mdr

Conclusion: Roadmap for a Viksit Bharat

1 https://www.livemint.com/opinion/columns/the-retreat-of-globalization-has-been-ill-timed-for-india-11580922457940.html

2 https://www.livemint.com/opinion/columns/the-retreat-of-globalization-has-been-ill-timed-for-india-11580922457940.html

3 https://www.businesstoday.in/latest/economy/story/india-to-become-third-largest-economy-in-the-next-three-years-says-jefferies-in-a-note-418454-2024-02-22

4 Kapoor, Amit & Debroy, Bibek (2019), GDP Is Not a Measure of Human Well-Being, Harvard Business Review

5 https://www.un.org/development/desa/dpad/publication/un-desa-policy-brief-no-153-india-overtakes-china-as-the-worlds-most-populous-country/#:~:text=In%20April%202023%2C%20India's%20population,to%20grow%20for%20several%20decades.

6 https://www.bcg.com/industries/education/client-success/improving-access-to-education-in-india

7 https://www.thehindubusinessline.com/news/national/gross-enrolment-ratio-improves-drop-out-rates-decline-economic-survey/article66454568.ece

8   https://www.ncbi.nlm.nih.gov/pmc/articles/PMC6175441/

9   https://sundayguardianlive.com/investigation/india-has-experienced-18-higher-growth-rates-in-modi-years

10   https://timesofindia.indiatimes.com/city/nagpur/the-urgency-of-urban-flooding-what-bengaluru-floods-2022-taught-us/articleshow/94212135.cms

11   https://www.ih21.org/aktuality/decentralisation-in-urban-india-beyond-the-73rd-74th-amendments

12   https://scroll.in/article/1032585/the-india-fix-crippled-city-governments-are-indias-biggest-governance-failure

13   https://pmc.ncbi.nlm.nih.gov/articles/PMC4621381/

14   https://www.publichealth.columbia.edu/research/programs/comparative-health-policy-library/india-summary

15   https://earth.org/environmental-issues-in-india/#:~:text=Illegal%20dumping%20of%20raw%20sewage,rivers%20and%20other%20water%20bodies.

16   https://eastasiaforum.org/2024/02/27/indias-thirst-for-improved-water-security/

17   https://www.bbc.com/news/world-asia-india-48744163

***

References

Nilekani Nandan, and Shah, Viral, Rebooting India: Realizing a Billion Aspirations Penguin Books India, 2015

Campbell-Johnson, Alan, *Mission with Mountbatten,* Jaico Publishing House, 1951

Strategy for New India@ 75, NITI Aayog, November 2018

Menon, V P, *The transfer of Power in India,* 1957 (Reproduced by Sani Panhwar, April 6, 2020)

Kakodkar, Anil, and Gangotra Suresh, *Fire and Fury, Transforming India's strategic Identity,* Rupa Publications, 2019

Tharoor Shashi, *An era of Darkness,* The British Empire in India, Aleph Book Company, New Delhi, 2016

Mosley, Leonard, *The last days of the British Raj,* Harcourt, Brace, & World, INC, Newyork,1962

Ravi, Shamika, *Accelerating Financial Inclusion in India,* Brookings India, March 2019

Raghavan, Srinath, *Fierce Enigmas: A History of the United States in South Asia,* Basic Books,2018

Alan Cambell-Johnson, *Mission with Mountbatten,* Macmillan Pub Co, January, 1985

Niti Aayog, *Strategy for New India@ 75*, 2018

Kakodkar, Anil &, Suresh Gangotra, Suresh, *Fire and Fury: Transforming India's Strategic Identity* Rupa Publications India, November 2019

Iyer, Parameswaran Iyer, *The Swachh Bharat Revolution: Four Pillars of India's Behavioural Transformation*, HarperCollins India, September 2019

Raghavan Srinath, Fierce Enigmas: *A History of the United States in South Asia*, Basic Books, December 2018

Menon, V P, *The Story of the Integration of the Indian States*, Longmans, Green and Co, London, 1955

Tharoor, Shashi, *An Era of Darkness*: *The British Empire in India*, Aleph Book Company, New Delhi, 2016

Mosley, Leonard, *The Last Days of the British Raj*, Harcourt, Brace & World, New York, 1961

Iyer, Parameswaran (Ed.), *The Swachh Bharat Revolution*: *Four Pillars of India's Behavioural Transformation*, Harper Collins India, 2019, Ministry of Education, Government of India, Report of the University Education Commission, 1962

***